The Times Bes.   .r 1998

The Times Best Sermons for 1998

Edited and Introduced by
Ruth Gledhill

Foreword by the Rt Revd Michael Turnbull

CASSELL

Cassell

Wellington House
125 Strand
London WC2R 0BB

370 Lexington Avenue
New York
NY 10017-6550

First published 1997
Reprinted 1998

British Library Cataloguing-in-Publication Data
A catalogue record for this book is available from the British Library.

ISBN 0-304-70220-X

Cover sculpture appears courtesy of Ros Stracey.

Typeset by Stephen Wright, The Rainwater Consultancy, Longworth, Oxfordshire
Printed and bound in Great Britain by Biddles Limited, Guildford and King's Lynn

Contents

Foreword

by the Bishop of Durham,
the Right Revd Michael Turnbull

It may come as a surprise that, in an age of information technology, the sermon continues as one of the most widespread and effective means of communication. Quite apart from the tens of thousands of sermons preached each week in our chapels and churches, a large proportion of the population hears sermons on special family, civic and national occasions. Sermons are frequently the subject of press coverage and many people can recall phrases and concepts which they heard in sermons long ago.

So what is the secret of the sermon's survival? First, it has to do with context. By definition a sermon is always preached in the setting of worship. The sermon is no isolated piece of oratory but is integral to a total act of wonder, exploration and reponse. Ruth Gledhill's column 'At Your Service' in *The Times* always fascinates me by the link that is made between the sermon and the total setting of building, worship and hospitality. The vast majority of sermons is preached to a local setting by someone who lives and works in the same environment as the hearers. A sermon always makes the links between a tradition and a contemporary context.

Second, the sermon has survived because of its content, starting as it does from the profound conviction that God has revealed himself to humankind. God being God, that has lasting implications for both the individual and society.

Listening to a sermon, then, demands more than just attention. It requires our participation in an activity in which preacher and hearer together discover a revelation addressed to a particular context. It is one of the frequent levellers of all preachers that people have heard something you are not conscious of saying. A universal truth has rung its own bells in the minds of the hearers and attached itself to the bundle of knowledge, experience and needs which is unique to each individual. There is no ready explanation of this other than God's communication at work.

In the light of this, judging whether a sermon is good or bad is futile. Its effectiveness will depend quite as much on the hearer as the preacher. At best, preaching is a two-way, communal process. A colleague once described preaching to a certain congregation as 'playing squash against a haystack'. There was no comeback, no resonance, no anticipation.

What is true of listening to sermons must also be true about reading them. The disadvantage is that the context of the preacher and reader are not the same as when both are in the same place and enjoying the same worship. Moreover, we lose the immediacy of the preacher, the inflections and gestures. The sermons in this book are designed to be spoken rather than written, to be heard rather than read.

Nevertheless, there are some advantages about reading a sermon. You can go at your own pace and refer backwards and forwards at will. You can check things out from other sources. It can still be a two-way process as we let our imagination provide the preacher's voice and the setting in which they preached. Above all, we need to remember that we are reading a sermon and not an essay.

Having pointed out the limitations of making judgements about sermons without, at the same time, judging the hearers, this collection of sermons is the result of a competition. Preachers and judges alike will admit to a certain arbitary subjectiveness in the process. But the great service which *The Times* and the College of Preachers have provided by setting up this now well-established competition is to draw to the public's attention the lasting value of the sermon. If we were to define the characteristics of an effective sermon, we might list them as follows: it should provide information and throw new light on familiar facts; it should seek to touch, by illustration and application, not only our minds but also our imaginations and emotions; it should invite a response which may take the form of further questioning and exploration, or a resolution by an act of will.

As you read these sermons (and I would suggest one at a time) you may like to apply these criteria, not so much perhaps to judge the sermon as to question the reader. *The Times* and the College of Preachers are greatly indebted to the large number of preachers, usually under pressure from their congregations, who have submitted themselves to the process of the competition and not least for allowing their sermons to be printed. The important thing is not whether they were shortlisted or reached the finals, but that the sermons were preached. We thank them for that and we hope they will understand that we are not so much scrutinising their sermons as submitting ourselves to examination by them.

†Michael Dunelm

Introduction

by Ruth Gledhill

According to one of our shortlisted preachers, Julian Templeton, God has been pushed to the margins of contemporary society. 'Preaching is vital in trying to bring God back from the margins and more into the centre of life,' he says.

A passionate belief in what they are trying to do, sometimes against enormous odds, was what came over most from this year's shortlisted preachers in *The Times*/College of Preachers Preacher of the Year award. A telephone survey of the preachers showed wide ranges in belief, style, methods of preparation and length of sermons. They had come to their Christian faith in diverse ways, some reluctantly, some by a gradual osmosis over the years, some by dramatic conversion experiences. But all shared a sense of the 'great commission', a determination and drive to use their ten or twenty minutes in the pulpit each week to make people think, to challenge, to offer comfort and consolation, and above all to make the 2,000-year-old Christian story relevant for this and the next millennium. The thirty preachers were aged between 28 and 81 years old. Nine were women, twenty were ordained and the other ten held lay offices in their church. Of the ordained preachers, two were religious: one a Dominican Blackfriar, the other a Benedictine. Although, as in the previous two years of the award, most were Anglican, there was a wide denominational spread this year, with a strong Free Church representation. Besides the seventeen Anglicans, there were four Methodists, two Presbyterians, two Roman Catholics, two Baptists, two from the United Reformed Church and one Congregationalist.

One preacher has trained himself never to use text or notes. Eleven use notes, although some of them have occasionally been called to preach off the cuff, or sometimes find themselves able to preach without an aid. The rest have a typed or handwritten text in front of them while they preach, although one never refers to it and simply has it there in case, while another has been trained to read from it but look as though she is not reading.

In keeping with their preaching tradition, the United Reformed Church ministers preached longest and spent longest in preparation, and Roman Catholics preached the shortest homilies. Anglicans, often with several churches to preach in each Sunday, tended to spend least time in preparation, although the Revd Harry Potter, who trained first as a cleric and is now a barrister, was most forthright, spending just half an hour in preparation. He made a convincing case that the length of time spent on preparation made no material difference to the quality of the end product.

Others spent twelve hours, fifteen hours, six hours, one-half to three hours, one week, several weeks, three weeks, a few days, four days finding a title and mulling it over, twelve hours over three days, two weeks, a few hours, a week, two hours, a week, a day, a week. Eight preachers said their sermons lasts 20 minutes, two go up to 25 minutes, two preach regularly for 4 minutes, one preaches each week for precisely 8 minutes, and the remainder preach for between 10 and 15 minutes. Congregation sizes vary from 4 people to as many as 800 or 1,000, with most between 40- and 120-people strong. The preachers might preach as little as three times a year (this was a woman who would quite clearly have liked to preach more but whose church benefits from a surfeit of retired ministers in its congregation), through to once a month, fortnightly, once a week to the awesome task faced by one vicar of delivering four sermons each Sunday.

Asked why they entered the competition, most did so because they were persuaded by members of their congregation who saw it advertised in *The Times*. But one, Dilys Owen-Quick, said: 'It was a challenge. And I really believed in what I had to say.' Michael Parker entered because he believes the competition encourages the art of the 'well-told sermon'.

Thomas Woodsend was sorting out his old sermons when he saw the advertisement in *The Times*, so he sent one in on the offchance. Another was already a successful competition winner and, having retired, relished the challenge of a new test. Brian Anker, a former Salvation Army captain, said: 'I entered because I wanted to find out just how I rate, whether I am failing myself or not. With the Salvation Army, after preaching I would usually appeal for some sort of response from individuals, and if they responded openly I knew I was being effective, but in the church there is not the same opportunity.'

Andrew Clitherow, entered 'by accident'. He does not buy a daily paper, but happened to see someone else's copy of *The Times*, open at the page where the entry coupon was published. 'I was glad to make the shortlist because I do not believe I preach very good sermons, although I try desperately hard,' he says. Roger Dawson entered after knocking over a pile of old sermons and happening to read one he liked as he sorted them out.

Dom Placid Meylink, a Benedectine prior, was entered by his secretary. He loves preaching. 'Preaching is proclaiming the word of God,' he pronounces, but insists that a preaching competition is 'silly'. By contrast, the other Catholic on the shortlist, Fr Edmund Hill, also a monk but a Dominican, thought entering the competion was a good thing to do. He said the award was 'a sensible idea'. Julian Templeton entered 'because I was interested to find out how what I do from week to week compares to what other people do'. Most had thought in some depth about the meaning of what they do. Brian Anker said preaching 'stimulates people into thinking more deeply about matters of faith and belief, and the really basic fundamentals of life.' Richard Buckley, who has to preach three times each Sunday, believes the sermon is an important educative tool in an age where fewer people read religious books. Some preach the same sermons twice, although most revise them. 'I consider it a discipline to rewrite before I repeat,' says Eric Burton, a Congregationalist. Richard Dormandy finds preaching 'thrilling' and loves the performance aspect. However, if it goes wrong, he feels 'awful and pathetic'. A good sermon will move and energize people in the same way that a great political speech will move them, he believes, and can even change lives. Andrew Clitherow compared preaching to 'giving birth', and said he finds it at once difficult and fulfilling. Roger Dawson enjoys the element of showmanship and freely admits to 'working the audience'.

One preacher, who asked that this particular comment should remain anonymous, confessed he is not keen on preaching at weddings. 'I see too many going wrong and that is always at the back of my mind,' he says. But he loves funerals: 'Then, they have arrived, and that is a strong message for eternal life.' Claire Wilson admits to enjoying the performance element of sermons and said she entered the award because of a competitive streak. 'I relish competitions,' she confessed.

Most in active parish work mentioned the strain of having to produce one or two sermons, week after week, with no let-up, and often for tiny congregations. Some, like Roger Dawson, preach between two and four sermons each Sunday. They might rework the same one for different congregations but make sure no congregation hears the same one twice. It is understandable that preachers might use the same sermon twice, given the hours that go into preparation, and when considering that one congregation might consist of no more than six people. Neville Manning, who runs a group of four parishes and preaches without notes or text, having committed a sermon to memory, regrets the pressure that having to preach too many sermons in a week can put on preparation time.

Gill Green, a member of the College of Preachers who responded to its invitation to enter, says: 'I do not know that preaching does much for people in terms of what I myself have to say, but it is an opportunity for the Holy Spirit to get in there and do some work for them.' Nearly all described the sermon in terms such as that it is an attempt to link the biblical message to contemporary life. Martin Camroux compared sermon preparation to 'painting the Forth Bridge'. No sooner is one week's over than the next week's looms. They know when the sermon is not working because people look bored, and, as one described, you can hear 'little shuffling noises'. Some were modest – such as Thomas Woodsend – who said he preaches 'until everybody has fallen asleep'. Surprisingly few used word processors, with most relying on handwritten notes or texts. Hardly any were on the Internet, but were familiar with the arcane mysteries of Bible commentaries, Latin and New Testament Greek.

Baptists such as Lorna Sivyour preach 'as the Holy Spirit moves'. Most follow the lectionary but a handful, such as the Revd Paul Walker in Sunderland, who preached an elegant sermon that put a convincing case for faith in the face of suffering and tragedy, like to preach from themes, or to take one gospel or book of the Bible and expound on it over several weeks.

However, preachers such as Joyce Critchlow cannot get enough of church or preaching. She has only missed one Sunday in 53 years at her local church and preaches regularly. 'It is the best calling of all because you are fulfilling the commission of Christ to spread the gospel,' she says. 'You should preach if you are feeling good or bad, because you are just an instrument in God's hands. If He called me to preach 20 out of 24 hours, I would do it.'

A Knock on the Window

Sermon written at the beginning of the year to be preached by the Revd Roy Allison at Verwood Methodist Church, Dorset on Sunday 12 October 1997.

The Revd Roy Allison, 58, was superintendent minister of the Methodist Church's South London Mission in Southwark but retired early due to ill health and now helps out in the Totnes Methodist circuit in Devon. He preaches about once a month in one of the seven village churches in the circuit. The largest, in Totnes itself, has a membership of 84. Mr Allison entered the 'Preacher of the Year' award after he was encouraged by his success in winning the 1995 'Economy in Government' competition, run by the Adam Smith Institute, which invites the public to float ideas for improving value for money in public services. The South London Mission had student and elderly residents and during his time there Mr Allison was also chairman of a convalescent and nursing home. The expertise he gained helped him to win the prestigious £1,500 first prize for his business plan outlining how money could be saved in long-term care. He has since seen some of his ideas incorporated into government thinking on the matter. A graduate of Fitzwilliam College, Cambridge, where he studied history and theology, Mr Allison has worked for the Methodist Church in Bristol, Plymouth, Salford and Manchester as well as London. He felt called to the ministry while still a schoolboy, and qualified as a local preacher as a sixth former. He usually preaches from the lectionary, beginning his preparation a week before he is due to deliver the sermon, and preaching from notes rather than a full script. He creates reams of paper during preparation, eventually collating his notes on the word processor given to him when he retired, and preaches usually for 20 minutes. 'I welcome the opportunity to convey the truth of God and the challenge of the gospel,' he says. 'There is a message of good news to convey, and I like to feel when I am preaching that I have something to

*say, and to convince people that this is what God is saying to them.
It is hard work to get it right but that is the challenge. I had been
thinking about the sermon I submitted to the award for a long time,
and it is something I really wanted to say.'*

Texts: Mark 14.7
Bible: New English Bible

A knock came on a Bristol charity shop window. A small boy
was standing there. The shop was closed, but the boy had
seen voluntary staff inside, sorting out the stock. You don't normally unlock a shop door just because a little boy knocks on the
window. But there was something appealing about the boy's face.
So they opened the door, to find a child in bare feet. Had they
any shoes that would fit him, he asked.

On another occasion, into that same church charity shop
came a woman carrying a brown paper parcel, which she held
tightly to her body. She was clearly in great distress. Gradually
the shop helpers encouraged her to show them the contents of
the parcel. Inside was a naked baby. Some people say real poverty
doesn't exist in Britain today. But it does.

One Christmas Eve, a mother called at the door of a London
church mission hall. She needed help. The family had received
their income support giro for about £200 a couple of days
before. It was to last a fortnight. The next day the husband
walked out with the money leaving the mother and five children
with nothing but heartache for Christmas. On another occasion
a young couple sought help because they were sleeping on the
street, and yet another because their only home was a battered
car. In each of these two cases the woman was pregnant.

My text is taken from the Gospel of St Mark, Chapter 14,
Verse 7. Jesus says: 'You have the poor among you always'. These
words were spoken in response to the criticism of a woman who
had poured costly perfume over the head of Jesus, as a gesture of
love. Surely it would have been better if the perfume had been
sold and the money given to the poor. It was worth about a year's
wage for a working man. This was no small amount.

So why did Jesus say that the woman should not be criticized?
It seems to show a somewhat callous concern for the needy. But
as usual, Jesus' first concern was for the person with whom he

had come face to face. 'Don't find fault with her,' he said. Her
intention was pure. Her devotion was clear. Her love demanded
expression. In other words: 'Recognise goodness when you see
it.' And he added: 'Wherever in all the world the Gospel is pro-
claimed, what she has done will be told as her memorial.' Indeed
the story, or one very similar to it, is told in each of the four
Gospels.

Jesus wanted to draw attention to the eternal value of true
devotion. But that was not all. He used the opportunity to challenge those who claimed to be concerned about the poor. If you
are truly concerned about them, reflect on why 'you have the
poor among you always'. And for the answer they needed to
recall the words of Deuteronomy:

> There will never be any poor among you if only you
> obey the Lord your God by carefully keeping these
> commandments which I lay upon you this day; for
> the Lord your God will bless you with greater pros-
> perity in the land which he is giving you to occupy as
> your patrimony.

(15.4–5)

In other words, the fact that poverty continues unabated is a sign
that God's Law is not being obeyed. And that's what you should
be doing something about. Be genuine about your concern for
the poor, not forgetting that Jesus said: 'Anything you do for one
of my brothers here, however humble, you do for me.'

So how has the Church responded to this challenge? Over the
centuries monasteries have provided hospitality, missionaries
have offered healthcare and education, and individual Christians
have led crusades against slavery, child labour and other oppres-
sive regimes. Such campaigns sometimes coincided with political
agendas espoused by others. But the Christians' motivation was
the challenge of the Gospel. You cannot truthfully claim to love
God if you do not love your brother or sister. True love is shown,
and does not remain simply the subject of conversation. God
demonstrated his love in sending his beloved son, who in turn
displayed God's love by his words and deeds. In our turn we
reflect our desire to share that love as we pray: 'Thy kingdom
come on earth'. And we show we mean what we say by seeking

to make the world what God intended it to be.

Jesus said that Christians should be the light of the world and the leaven in society, continuing his own ministry outlined in his manifesto announced to the people of Nazareth. (Luke 4). This included the commission taken from Isaiah 61: 'The Lord . . . has sent me to announce good news to the poor.' The question that must be asked is whether Christians are continuing to fulfil that calling.

Some Christians think that providing assistance for the poor is the task of politicians. They have the power to create legislation to enable wealth to cascade down the generations. Or they can legislate to transfer wealth from the rich to the poor, if they have a mind to do so. The Church, they say, should confine itself to spiritual matters. And it is certainly true that the Church has the privileged task of bringing people to know Jesus Christ as their personal Lord and Saviour. But is such an opt-out the true Christian way?

Many Christians say it is not. Politicians have their job to do, but it is the Church's task to challenge and cajole our democratically elected leaders at every opportunity. And it is true that politicians should be reminded of their moral responsibility to serve all of the people all of the time. But is such lobbying enough?

Other Christians recognize that the Church should go further and stand by those in need. So the Church has appointed professional staff to mission alongside the poor. And bishops have recently been pictured talking to the homeless as they sell copies of the *Big Issue*. But is this response appropriate, let alone adequate? Perhaps the answer is to be found in the response made by a disadvantaged woman to a researcher: 'If there's one thing I hate it's being lived among.'

Just like anyone who recognizes their need, whether it be spiritual, moral or material, they want their life to be changed. And when Jesus taught us to pray: 'Thy will be done on earth as it is in heaven', he didn't expect us then to sit back and do nothing about it. If the poor of today are to have good news announced to them, it is our responsibility to do it. And while the 'good news' begins with the fact that God loves each one of us, and Jesus died for each of us, it does not end with words. The Word is made flesh. It is God's purpose that everyone should have the opportunity to share in the good things of life. And Christians are called to share in the fulfilling of that purpose. The parable of the sheep and the goats should leave us in no doubt. Instead of pyramid selling, it is pyramid giving, for those who experience God's love will want to share it.

And it is those in greatest need who require the greatest help – the poor, the outcast and the friendless. And as if to make the point irrefutable, these were the sort of people Jesus himself helped and befriended. There's nothing wrong in attempting to persuade politicians to ensure the poor are properly provided for. But that's not what Jesus had in mind. When he was faced with a crowd of 5,000 hungry people, the disciples wanted Jesus to send them away to the farms and villages around to buy food. Jesus said: 'Feed them yourselves.' 'We can't,' they said. 'We haven't got the resources.' And what happened? A boy contributed his lunch, and as a result of that gift, which Jesus blessed, adequate resources were made available.

The principles at work here are eternal. Resources do exist to meet people's needs. What is required is first, the key to make those resources available, and second, the desire to turn the key in the lock which is holding back those resources. Some people say they don't believe in miracles. So they would never accept that Jesus turned water into wine at Cana-in-Galilee. But if the farmers around Bordeaux failed to do this each year, many wine drinkers would be bitterly disappointed.

Belief in miracles does not require us to imagine that every time we face a crisis, God sends an army of angels to get us out of trouble. Angels may well have come to support Jesus after his temptations in the wilderness. But at the crucifixion, despite taunts that Elijah would appear to release him, Jesus was left there to die. Jesus had previously pointed to the fact that a seed needs to die in order to produce fruit that is alive. So death and resurrection are part of the natural world too. The key is to see the world as God's world, created by him and exhibiting his principles and purpose. The key is turned by our faith in those truths. And that faith produces a deeper and more perceptive understanding of events.

The woman who poured costly ointment on Jesus was showing a love which, if expressed universally, would eradicate poverty. The gesture of selling the perfume and giving the proceeds to the poor might provide temporary alleviation of need. But it is the characteristics of love and devotion demonstrated by the woman through her gift to Jesus which would truly fulfil the Law of God and banish poverty for ever. The poor remain among you, said Jesus, because you don't have that love. But if you were to follow the example of this woman, the poor would be poor no more.

Don't Leave it to Them

Sermon preached by Brian Anker at St Martin's Church, Cambridge, on Sunday 12 January 1997.

Brian Anker, 60, was a Salvation Army officer for most of his life, serving in eight different corps over a period of 16 years, and reaching the rank of captain. Sadly, he had to leave his officership when his first wife left him. Previously, he was in the Royal Electrical and Mechanical Engineers, and also spent three years collecting water rates for the Metropolitan Water Board in London. He can name the precise day he was converted, 18 November 1958. 'I had been going round with a gang,' he says. 'It was the teddy-boy era. I could never afford the real teddy-boy gear, but I just used to behave like one. I would swagger around and get into the occasional fight. One day, we were challenged by a lady Salvationist who said we didn't have the nerve to go to a meeting. So we did. After going for a few weeks, the whole gang of us went forward one evening and became Christians.' He met his second wife, Margaret, at the Cambridge church he now attends, and has found work running a small home for adults with learning disabilities. Meanwhile, he has qualified as a reader, preaching once or twice a month. 'To prepare, I look at the set readings from the lectionary until one grabs my attention, then I home in on it and keep reading the same passage until the sermon starts to develop its own structure.' He spends some time each day over two weeks thinking about it, building up to two hours a day, when he starts to put it down on paper. 'I actually get really excited about what the passage is saying to me and then, hopefully, I share that excitement with the congregation on the day.'

Texts: Isaiah 61.4

> They will rebuild the ancient ruins and restore the places long devastated.

Bible: New International Version

My aim is to encourage ordinary people to take responsibility for rebuilding and restoring the foundations of faith and the structure of moral values of our society. How many of you watched what was advertised as a debate about the monarchy? How many of you switched off when it degenerated into a slanging match? I hear that the result was a two-thirds majority for retention; possibly because the alternative of a professional politician as head of state sounds even worse. The monarch, our head of state in Britain, holds the title 'Defender of the Faith' although the next in line, Prince Charles, would prefer to be considered 'Defender of Faith' in order to include other religions.

There is plenty of evidence that faith has not been very well defended in Britain for some time now. While the Queen herself has tried to secure the boundaries, some members of the Royal Family have probably done more harm than good in that respect. Some maverick clergy must have caused her to wonder whose side they were on and many of the policies adopted by politicians of successive governments and varying political bias have done much to erode the faith and morality of our nation. There are many who long for a rebuilding and restoring of faith and the moral standards based on religious faith but it is hard to see who will carry out that rebuilding.

In the prophecy of Isaiah we have heard the promise: 'They will rebuild the ancient ruins and restore the places long devastated.' The writer of this prophesy saw a strong link between the symbols of faith, the moral outworking of faith and inward faith.

The following selected verses from Isaiah 58 demonstrate this.

> On the day of your fasting you do as you please and exploit all your workers. Your fasting ends in quarrelling and strife, and striking each other with wicked fists.
>
> (vv. 3–4)

> Is not this the kind of fasting I have chosen: to loose the chains of injustice and untie the cords of the yoke, to set the oppressed free and break every yoke? Is it not to share your food with the hungry and pro-

vide the poor wanderer with shelter – when you see
the naked to clothe him, and not to turn away from
your own flesh and blood?

(vv. 6–7)

If you do away with the yoke of oppression, with the
pointing finger and malicious talk, and if you spend
yourself on behalf of the hungry and satisfy the needs
of the oppressed, then your light will rise in the darkness, and your night will become like the noonday.

(vv. 9–10)

Your people will rebuild the ancient ruins and will
raise up the age-old foundations; you will be called
Repairer of Broken Walls, Restorer of Streets with
Dwellings.

(v. 12)

When we look around at the modern buildings of our towns and
cities we see that streets with dwellings are given a lower priority
than the cathedrals of commerce and consumerism that domi-
nate the skylines. They symbolize a morality of exploitation and
abuse by the rich and powerful of the greater part of the population and a faith only in materialism and humanism.

The message of Jesus was firmly established in continuity with
that of Isaiah when early in his public ministry he read in the
synagogue at Nazareth a version of the opening of Isaiah 61:
From Luke 4.18–19, we read that he said:

The Spirit is upon me because he has anointed me to
preach good news to the poor. He has sent me to proclaim freedom for the prisoners and recovery of sight
for the blind, to release the oppressed, to proclaim
the year of the Lord's favour.

He began his subsequent talk by saying to them: 'Today this
scripture is fulfilled in your hearing.' His call to his fellow Jews
to rebuild their spiritual foundations was inextricably entwined

9

with a call to social as well as personal moral values. He also pointed them towards the Temple as a symbolic focus for spirituality and morality. His dramatic act of turning out from that place of worship the commerce that had infiltrated it was followed up by his declaration that the Temple would be torn down and rebuilt. It was a twisted version of this statement that was used in his trial before the Sanhedrin and was crucial in their case against him.

The need of our society for a spiritual and moral rebuilding is acknowledged by many. But who will do the rebuilding? We tend to demand an initiative from a poorly defined 'them'. At the back of our minds are the wealthy who have financial and material resources. There were outstanding philanthropists in Victorian Britain but today philanthropy is staged as a publicity stunt that ends up with the wealthy even better off and the poor just as needy and heavily dependent.

There are the politicians who have the political power to redistribute wealth. With a general election approaching the politicians and their publicists are approaching with sound bites and slogans to tap into that perception of need. They say that they will rebuild the ancient ruins and restore the places long devastated. But past experience gives us little cause for confidence in their promises.

There are talented people who have abilities far beyond those of ordinary mortals like you and me. But mostly those talents are used to inflate their egos and their bank balances. There are the visionaries, religious leaders and philosophical thinkers whose minds could be freed to envisage earthly utopias or heaven on earth. But increasingly they are drawn into maintaining and organizing instead of enlightening and enthusing.

Who did Isaiah mean when he said: 'They will rebuild the ancient ruins and restore the places long devastated.' Not the wealthy, the powerful, the talented or visionaries. He turned popular conceptions upside down because he tells us who they are at the start of the chapter.

> The Spirit of the Sovereign Lord is upon me because the Lord has anointed me to preach good news to the poor. He has sent me to bind up the broken hearted, to proclaim freedom for the captives and release from darkness for the prisoners.

The poor, the broken hearted, the captives, the prisoners in darkness. Isaiah prophesied a world turned upside down and a topsy-turvy world is frightening. The rich, powerful, talented and visionaries are terrified of allowing others to have control, and those at the other end of those scales are terrified of having the responsibility.

And in the middle are people like us with some financial security, voting power, moderate abilities and vision if only we open our eyes. For us the topsy-turvy world requires that we change the way we look at this society we inhabit; change the way we think about it, in fact repent and think again. Such a radical rethink only becomes possible when we believe the good news, that the creator of this world has entered it in power and remains active in it to empower those who believe.

People rather like us are the ones God can use to rebuild the ruins of faith, restore the moral values of society and establish the Church, the body of Christ as a focus for faith. Jesus called ordinary people to be his disciples and the early Church consisted mostly of the lower orders of society. The example of his life and the power provided through his death turned the world upside down as Isaiah prophesied. We do not entirely fulfil all the criteria but in each of us is something of some of them.

Poverty is relative. Even the poorest of us here has more than the richest of the thousands crowded into refugee camps. These days I have a greater financial stability than I have ever had before and it is very comfortable. My incentive for change is in danger of being eroded. My inclinations to restore and rebuild could be lost.

Does God require us to become poor? Possibly he does and perhaps not, but we must never lose touch with the poor. The time I spend at the Salvation Army community centre helps me keep in touch with the reality of poverty. We should not pity the poor but rather allow their poverty to anger us as it did Jesus.

A broken heart is not always worn on the sleeve and I am aware of the emotional distress some of you have endured and are enduring. If you have never had your heart broken it could be that you have so heavily armoured it that the needs of others cannot touch it.

My lack of grief at the deaths of my father, my older sister and my two younger brothers has sometimes in the past caused me to wonder whether I have a heart. Without a heart that can be broken you cannot love. The Tin Man wanted to ask the Wizard of Oz for a heart in order to love. The Wizard pointed out that tears of grief when he thought his friends were dead showed that he had one all the time. To find reassurance about my heart I had to rediscover the times when I have grieved and value them as signs of strength, not despise myself for weakness. Only the broken hearted care enough to rebuild and restore. The rest exploit what lies in the ruins.

Captivity can be within a body that cannot carry out the desires of the heart. We must be wary of thinking too much about our limitations. For twenty-five years I persevered at learning to play the guitar. A few years ago I gave my instrument away to a student with more talent for music and in doing so liberated time and energy to concentrate on the abilities God created me with and the gifts he was waiting to pour out through his Spirit.

The darkness of imprisoned minds can negate our incentives, longings and abilities. We might say that we long for leaders with vision but are only prepared to accept the leadership of visionaries who lead us along the limited paths of our prejudices. It is not vision in our leaders that we should cry for but the light of God's message that we should open up to. It takes courage to accept the truth that it is we who are called to rebuild the ancient ruins and restore the places long devastated.

The peace process in Northern Ireland is not the work of the wealthy, the politicians, the talented or the visionaries. It is often frustrated by them. It is ordinary people like us who have the poverty, broken hearts, limited talents and blind faith who do the work. Isaiah 62.12 says:

> They will be called the Holy People, the Redeemed of the Lord, and you will be called the Sought After, the City No Longer Deserted.

Mark 1.15 says:

> The Kingdom of God is near. Repent and believe the good news.

If you accept the challenge of both Isaiah and Jesus, pray:

Almighty God, creator of this world and lover of all that is in it, we confess that we have too long failed you by leaving the responsibility of rebuilding and restoration to others.

Forgive us Lord and encourage us to take on the tasks you set before us. May we become the Repairers of Broken Walls, the Restorers of Streets with Dwellings, Cities No Longer Deserted, a Holy People, the Redeemed of the Lord, the Sought After.

May we become for our society the symbol of what can be. May we seek to order our lives by the eternal values you have shown us. May we have deep and abiding faith in what we can be by the power of your Holy Spirit promised and sent through your Son, Jesus Christ our Lord.

God Calls Us to Respond

A sermon preached by Gillian Belford at a Women's World Day of Prayer service at Sands Methodist Church, Appleby, Cumbria, on Friday 1 March 1996.

Gillian Belford, 50, whose husband David is a vet in a country practice in Cumbria, trained as a nurse and became a ward sister before she married. She was brought up in the Church but stopped going when she left her north London home and started work. In 1984, at 36, she had a dramatic conversion experience when some students from a Bible college came through her part of Cumbria on the national 'Mission England' project. As a family, Gillian, her husband and three children had been attending church intermittently. 'But then this girl came from the Bible college and she just had something I wanted. Everything changed absolutely and completely. I stopped being frustrated and rather bored by the limitations of my own set-up. I started on this wonderful adventure of life with Jesus.' Four years later, Gillian felt personally called by God to preach. She was with a group of Christian musicians meeting for worship, and they needed a preacher. 'God said to me: "That is you",' she relates. 'I squirmed. I was tearful. The others were a bit hesitant, because they were Baptists and not used to women preachers.' She went ahead, trained as a local preacher in the Methodist Church and now preaches on alternate Sundays. 'To prepare, I spend a lot of time in prayer with the Lord,' she says. 'I wait on the Lord, for what I feel he is calling me to say. I can work under pressure but I would rather prepare over a few weeks. I do a lot of reading through the scriptures to see how God is speaking to me. Once I've got going, I like to write it down. When I am preaching, I am firing on four cylinders. It is very precious to me. I love to share the good news of Jesus. Though I use notes, people are praying for me as I preach and God is giving me more freedom to deliver his message.'

Texts: Revelation 3.20; Jeremiah 1.4–10; Luke 1.26–38

Here I stand, knocking at the door.

Bible: Good News

God calls us to respond. Is God knocking at the door of your heart? Is he still waiting to enter for the very first time? Not long after I was converted in February 1984 I heard a preacher say: 'A lot of women won't be in heaven. They are holding back from saying yes to Jesus as Saviour, Lord and the only way to eternal life, because of their husbands.'

Has someone in your life got his foot behind the door of your heart? Mary was a virgin, promised in marriage to a man named Joseph when God sent the Angel Gabriel to her. She anticipated being Joseph's wife and bearing his children but she did not let Joseph's foot rest behind the door of her heart when God knocked.

Is God knocking at the door of your heart and mine? Is he still waiting to enter, for the very first time, into some closed off area of our life? We mustn't leave Jesus in a compartment marked Sunday or Duty. No. Jesus wants to permeate our very existence moment by moment. His intimate calling is a wonderful privilege, but few respond wholeheartedly.

How often we hide behind the neat apparel of modest living, cautious good deeds and conforming behaviour, when Jesus is knocking at the door of our heart, wanting to fling it lovingly off its hinges. Is God trying to get your attention? Is Jesus on the doorstep of each of our hearts, calling at this moment through an almost closed door?

Don't be afraid. As he did with Mary, God comes to bless. His call brings his greetings, his encouragement and his purpose. God not only calls us to respond individually to the saving grace of his son, but also to the tasks of his saving grace. We can't send a husband, a friend, or anyone else, to answer for us. It has to be you, it has to be me, when God calls, for his call is not only divine, it is specific. Specific to you, specific to me, and specific to the building of his Kingdom here on earth. Do you know God loves you and me every bit as much as he did Mary? Every bit as much as he did the people of Haiti? We are each special, and even if you and I were the only people on earth Jesus would have died to save us from our sins and risen again, to give us eternal life in him. He's alive, hallelujah.

God's greetings, God's encouragement and God's purpose became apparent to Mary as she listened, as she questioned, and then as she responded wholeheartedly in trust and obedience. What God asked was huge, it was totally life changing. From that moment of saying: 'I am the Lord's servant', Mary left village obscurity and the strict code of Jewish conduct and let God lovingly thrust her into worldwide eternal view.

How many layers of modern life is Jesus trying to get through in order to reach your heart and mine, and gain a total response? Our families, our friends, our jobs, our possessions, our personal ambitions or difficulties, must not stop us from responding to God. Mary's plans before the Angel Gabriel arrived were good, no one could doubt that, and if she had proceeded with them following God's call, they would have still seemed good in the eyes of Joseph, her family and friends, but not in God's eyes. He had called her to a specific task at a specific time. How often what we do what is good, but it is not the best. The best is always in God's way and God's timing. God calls us to respond like Mary, to be listening, to be questioning, and then to be wholeheartedly trusting and obedient.

When Haiti was discovered in 1492 by Christopher Columbus, he named it the Garden of Eden, a lovely link with us here in the Eden valley, hundreds of years on and hundreds of miles away. Our terrain and theirs are beautiful. Add the word tropical to the Haiti climate, and we have a description of an earthly paradise. But within this apparent paradise is much turbulence and abuse of land and people. Indeed the frequent cry of *anm'wé*, danger, haunted the opening part of this service and readily conveys the desperation of the Haitian women as they call upon God and us to respond to the needs of their country. If all this trouble seems far off, remote, it isn't. Behind the doors of many comfortable looking homes here in the Eden valley, there is much pain, and plenty of folk silently crying their own *anm'wé*, but who will listen?

We who know God's love and power in our own lives and are called by him to respond to the needs of our neighbour, to draw alongside individuals and listen: 'First, as we take time with God in prayer, Bible study and worship, we learn to listen to him. As we listen Lord, we pray, Master speak to us today.' Be confident in God, he will call us, and he will use us if we hear and respond.

Second, be confident that God will show you and me who to draw alongside, so many need a listening ear in this age of hurried activity. Third, be confident that God will equip us in this outreach. The only ability that God wants is our availability, he'll do the rest. To any person crying *anm'wé*, a listening ear is a loving ear, a listening ear is a patient ear, and hopefully our listening ear is also a confidential ear and a prayerful ear. And with that attentive ear comes God's love and power in the shape of you and me.

Jeremiah was Judah's prophet, and Mary the mother of our Lord Jesus Christ. You and I can be a friend and help people who need us. Each role is important, if it is the one God calls us to respond to. We are required to listen, to be questioning the whys and wherefores of God's directions and then to be whole-heartedly trusting and obedient.

Jesus tells us in John 14, Verse 21:

> Those who accept my commandments and obey them are the ones who love me. My father will love those who love me, I too will love them, and reveal myself to them.

God calls us to respond, often with prayer, to the needs of those in far-off lands such as Haiti, but ultimately for most of us, our first call is to shine for Jesus here in our homes, here in our churches, and here in our community. Not one or two out of these three, but all three. God has placed you and me in the Appleby area for his purposes. He planned that we should live here, and we must seek to work within his plan to the glory of Jesus.

'Do not conform yourselves to the standards of this world,' as Paul tells us in Romans 12.2, 'but let God transform you inwardly by a complete change of your mind. Then you will be able to know the will of God, what is good and what is pleasing to him, and is perfect.' God is calling us as Christian women to pull together, not just one March day each year, but every day, as we live and move among relatives, friends and acquaintances who need our listening ears.

I have a treasured and wise friend who says that if something is of God, it will, as we pray and reflect on it, become sweeter and sweeter. If God has touched your heart today, if he is calling you to be a listening friend to that sad-looking teenager, that bright but brittle neighbour, that person who appears to have every-thing except Jesus, he will confirm that call in some specific way. Watch, wait, pray and listen. God does call us to respond, every-one of us, but always he calls us to respond in his way and in his time. Let us as Christian women, on this Women's World Day of Prayer, be aware of our glorious privilege and responsibility, as we daily ask him to:

> Open our eyes. Lord,
> we want to see Jesus —
> to reach out and touch Him.
> and say that we love Him.
> Open our ears, Lord,
> and help us to listen:
> O, open our eyes, Lord,
> we want to see Jesus.

Giving for Independence

Sermon preached by Richard Buckley at a service for Christian Aid at St Peter and St Paul's Church, Todwick, South Yorkshire, on Sunday 15 September 1996.

The Revd Richard Buckley, 54, is shortly leaving parish ministry in the Church of England to work full time for Christian Aid. Ordained at 23, the minimum age possible, he sometimes says he has never had a 'proper job'. Growing up in north Devon in a Christian family, he has always had a strong faith and thought 'why not me?' when contemplating the priesthood at the age of 14. He has been vicar of Holy Trinity, Wentworth, in the Sheffield diocese for six years, as well as working as area co-ordinator for Christian Aid. Richard, whose wife Sylvia is a supply teacher, preaches three times in two churches each Sunday so, unsurprisingly, he uses one sermon twice. 'I might as well be honest,' he says, 'I feel my sermons are somewhat slapdash sometimes. Being a good Anglican, I usually try and start from the lectionary readings. I find the College of Preachers fellowship papers extremely useful in supplying good ideas. I often try and personalize a sermon with my own stories. Preaching helps me to sort out my own ideas, and I hope it is helpful to people in developing their faith and perhaps expanding their horizons.' He confesses it can be hard to produce two sermons a week, every week, for 50 weeks a year. 'It does get somewhat routine.' But he still thinks the sermon has a vital place in the church. 'Most members of church congregations do not read a great deal of religious books,' he says. 'If there were no sermons, their faith might remain undeveloped.'

I should have been here more than six months ago, but I was snowed off. I'm grateful to David for reissuing the invitation, to Joan and Roy for the wonderful way that they organize the Christian Aid collection in Todwick every year, and to you all for your giving and your support.

Marjorie Lewis-Cooper is the General Secretary of the Caribbean Council of Churches. She spoke to a group of Christian Aid workers this week and reminded us of something which, in our business, we often forget – that all we do is grounded in prayer. And that prayer is essential in order to make sure that whatever we do is the will of God. I am reassured that it is after hearing again today's three Bible readings. Scripture speaks so clearly on this – you cannot pretend to love God unless you love your brother and sister here on earth first. Would that I had the wings of eloquence to make each of these passages live. I can only try.

It's amazing how often one can read a story and not notice something. 'A poor man named Lazarus used to be brought to the rich man's door, hoping to eat the scraps that fell from his table.' I never noticed that he was brought to the door, and surely that means Lazarus was disabled. I can picture now in my mind's eye the woman with the grossly swollen leg on the pavement outside Madras townhall, or the frail old people on the streets of the prosperous town of Cochabamba in Bolivia – and, incidentally, the beggar in a wheelchair in that richest of cities, San Francisco. All reduced to begging by disability.

Maybe once they were all young and fit and able to earn a day's pay. And then the hammer blow fell – a stroke, an accident, or just advancing years – leaving them unable to work. In a country which still has welfare provision, it is hard to understand how exposed such poor are. As a prayer I used this week says, 'Open our eyes, Lord, to a world in which even the crumbs under the table are taken from the mouths of the poor.'

Lazarus is not alone. In the early 1980s the international price of tin collapsed, literally overnight, due to the failure of a City of London scheme of price maintenance. City financiers soon recovered. But in the high Andean alti-plano of Bolivia, mines which had supported, paid and housed whole communities closed for ever. The effect of such a hammer blow is very similar to that of sudden disablement. In the same way it stops people working, it stops them earning, and it makes them unable to support themselves or their families. There were thousands and thousands of Lazaruses up there in the mining towns. And all brought about by a cause as much beyond their control as illness or accident.

What has happened to these people? There is no future for them in their mountain homes. So many of them have migrated to kinder valley environments, such as Cochabamba, which has a beautiful Spanish colonial centre, modern multi-storey office blocks and – on a hill outside the town – a dominating statue of Christ even larger than the famous one in Rio de Janiero. But of course the new residents don't get to live in these favoured places, but build shanty towns of mud brick on the outskirts. But they cannot all pick up crumbs from rich men's tables by begging. One solution was evident outside our hotel, where women stood on the pavement just after dawn waiting to be hired as domestic help – not a regular job, just for the day. That isn't far removed from Lazarus's position. People who have worked and supported their families deserve better.

We've heard a lot in Britain over the past ten years about the importance of the small business sector and how self-employment can take up some of the slack caused by redundancies. Bolivia is no different. But it's not too easy to get started, and that's where Christian Aid money can help by providing start-up capital or finance for new equipment.

Now don't imagine anything very large scale, or offices full of computers. We're talking grass roots here. For instance, one of my most memorable mornings in South America was spent in a rubbish collection depot. Not the municipal one, but a small yard which was the depot of a co-operative – that's its name, 'Mespal'. About a dozen of the shanty town dwellers have formed this co-op. They have a contract with the town to clean their township, which is spotless, absolutely spotless, when compared to the general filth typical of Peruvian townships. The co-op members wear these caps and smart grey overalls and patrol their area on large luggage tricycles, if you can visualize what I mean. My colleague and I were there to dedicate a new addition paid for by Christian Aid, which was an aluminium smelter to melt down scrap pots and pans, so providing extra income for the co-op. We had a super morning, with a warm welcome, speeches, the presentation of this certificate – and beer to wet the smelter's head! The people were so thrilled with what they were achieving, which was no less than independence, freeing themselves from the chains of Lazarus. It was a privilege for me to stand beside such people, and that, metaphorically, is what Christian Aid does with your help – it stands beside the poor to assist them to escape from poverty and dependence.

Sometimes the word escape is rather more literal. Negeshua started working in a brickworks at the age of 5. Two years later he was sold – as are many Indian children – to the owner of a carpet factory, who kept him working 12 or 13 hours a day in a dark room with little food, 7 days a week. At the age of 14 Negeshua was able to help some younger children to escape, but he himself was recaptured. Because he refused to tell the owner where the children had gone, he was tied up in darkness, gagged so that no one would hear his screams, and his body was burnt all over with hot irons. A Christian-Aid-funded organization that seeks to help such child slaves was alerted by other children. Negeshua was rescued and taken to a rest home. For three weeks he said nothing, until a colleague came on a visit. The other children were celebrating, singing, dancing. Negeshua sat there at first, showing no animation. Then he stood, and everyone looked at him; that went on for 10 minutes, with Negeshua evidently wanting to speak, but not being able to. Eventually he began not to speak, but to sing, just two lines – 'Never weep for a single moment in your life, always live with a smile in your heart.' He did speak a bit more, saying: 'If you have not helped anyone, you are not fully human.' How could one so ill-treated, so denied human kindness all his life, speak thus?

To stand alongside him, and alongside the rubbish collectors of Cochabamba, is indeed a God-given privilege. He calls us to do it. 'There will always be some who are poor and in need,' ancient Israel was told, 'and so I command you to be generous to them.' The parable of Lazarus is complete in itself; it needs no embroidering. And the apostle John adds, 'Christ gave his life for us; we, then, ought to give our lives for our brothers. Our love should not just be words and talk; it must be true love, which shows itself in action.'

God help us not only to talk – as it is so easy for me to do – but to act by standing alongside those who need, for a time, our strength to support their own. May God bless you in your prayers and in your doing.

Giving a Good Reception

Sermon preached twice by Eric Burton, first at the Congregational Centre, Nottingham, on Sunday 1 October 1995, then at St Mary's Church, Riseholme, Lincolnshire, on Sunday 28 January 1996.

The Revd Eric Burton, 71, is a retired Congregational minister who trained at Manchester University after leaving the RAF. Ordained at 26, he served in Essex, Devon, Gloucestershire, East Sussex and finished up in Leicester for 11 years. He has also contributed to religious broadcasts on national and local radio. In retirement he still travels around, preaching and serving Congregational churches. He has also been elected to the parochial church council of his local Anglican church, and edits their parish newsletter. He was brought up in a Christian home, but it was the things he saw in the war that persuaded him to go into the ministry. He preaches up to three times a month, and enjoys having more time to prepare than when he was in full-time ministry. 'Preaching is part of the commission of a Christian, a form of witness,' he says. 'The age we live in now tends to be on the visual side, so the use of illustrations like Jesus' parables is desirable.' Sometimes, he will preach the same sermon twice. 'But if I do this I always revise it,' he says. 'I make it a discipline to sit down and rewrite before I repeat.'

Texts: John 1. 11–12a
Bible: Authorised Version

Do you get a good reception? Radio listeners will know what I mean by that question. If you do not get a good reception, you find it hard to enjoy listening. But do you give a good reception? That is the question I am asking this morning.

To give a good reception is essential to joyful living. In so many things we're intended to be at the receiving end. Hear again these words from the gospel read earlier in this service: Jesus Christ 'came unto his own, and his own received him not. But as many as received him, to them gave he the power (that is the privilege, or right) to become the sons of God'.

While we do well to remember the words of the Lord Jesus, how he said, 'It is more blessed to give than to receive,' it is sometimes harder to be a receiver than a giver. The very nature of God the creator is to provide, so we are primarily at the receiving end, not only now as you listen to this sermon, but in everything. The apostle Paul asked the question: 'What do you possess that was not given you?' We might do well to go on asking that of ourselves. It's a great thing to discover that real wealth lies in things that are given.

Part of our problem is that we so like to be independent. But the independence does not always spring from commonsense or Christian grace and deprives us of much that is necessary to life. Some people who are so grimly bent on doing good might well heed the not entirely facetious question: If you are in this world to help others, what are the others here for? C. S. Lewis wrote that there are people who live for others, but that you can tell the others by the 'hunted look' in their eyes.

How much easier it can be to give a service rather than to receive help; to give advice rather than take it. Ask any invalid or physically handicapped person. Elizabeth Sheppard-Jones, a paraplegic confined to a wheelchair, makes this point about the grace of receiving so effectively in her book, *I Walk on Wheels*. She found she was unable even to post her own letters because as soon as she tried to do so she had so many offers to help her post them that it would have been selfish of her to refuse. She came to the conclusion that it was a bad thing to bear resentment over being helped with anything, and that when she needed help she should accept it willingly and graciously.

This applies just as much to those of us who do not live in wheelchairs. We may see from the Gospels that Jesus did not despise receiving. He accepted the hospitality of the home of Mary and Martha and the costly oil from the alabaster box of a prostitute who wanted forgiveness. He made use of a boy's picnic lunch of loaves and fishes and borrowed a fisherman's boat. He borrowed a penny and was even pleased to be given a donkey! Jesus began his earthly life in a borrowed stable and ended part one in a borrowed grave.

Jesus does not ask us to be independent. He comes to those who have a thirst for the spiritual with the offer, 'I am living water', yet graciously requests of a despised foreign woman, 'Give me a drink.' He comes to those who are hungry for the only way of life which is meaningful, saying, 'I am the bread of life', yet speaks memorably about 'when I was hungry you gave me food'. The gospel records of Jesus ooze with the grace. Or, if we may put it this way, for what he had received the Lord was truly thankful.

Jesus gave a good and gracious reception. That is more than he received. 'He came unto his own, and his own received him not.' That text describes his coming in a unique way. It is the coming of a traveller expecting to receive a good welcome as he comes to his rightful home. As we try to apply the text to ourselves, the underlying question must persist: do we give a good reception?

But to turn your radio on is not enough in itself. That won't get you the best possible reception. You have to tune in to the right waveband. Even that's not enough, unless you are content just to have a background noise. Something is required of you as well as your radio. To get the best reception you must listen.

No less is required if we are to hear the Word of God. Jesus ends his parable of the sower with the words: 'Listen, then if you have ears to hear with!' We have to listen and listen intelligently at that. 'The Word became flesh' in Jesus. Think or that – the Word of God became animated. Sound and now vision too, in Jesus. So, 'the Word became flesh; he came to dwell among us' on our wavelength, our channel. 'He came unto his own' and he got a bad reception. Is it any better now? Are we giving God in Jesus Christ a hearing? Giving a good reception requires listening intently and intelligently.

The text adds: 'But as many as received him'. That means anybody and everybody. It includes us in! The Christian way of life is a gift God offers to us. The emphasis is not so much on our doing. This may be a point worth noting for those who have almost given up the strain and the struggle. The emphasis is rather on our accepting – giving a good reception to – what God in Jesus Christ offers. A commoner cannot approach a king with the offer of friendship. If there is ever to be such a friendship, it must begin with an approach from the king. It is so with God and us. Without this offering from God you cannot achieve or earn salvation, however strenuous your efforts.

There is the other side of the coin too: 'As many as received him'. We must take what God offers in Jesus Christ if we are to possess it. So binding are the laws protecting the rights and privileges of the private citizen in this country that not even the Queen may enter anybody else's home uninvited. Imagine Her Majesty waiting on your doorstep for a word of welcome! The gospel situation is like that. God's gift awaits us. If anything is to happen we must give a good reception. Jesus breathed on the disciples, saying, 'Receive the Holy Spirit.' That offer still holds now. On his travels, the apostle Paul found a number of converts of whom he asked: 'Did you receive the Holy Spirit when you became believers?' That question still holds now. They of old had to say, 'No, we have not even heard that there is a Holy Spirit.' We have heard! Paul adds: 'As many as are led by the Spirit of God, they are the sons of God . . . ye have received the Spirit of adoption.'

In a home for deprived children a man and his wife had long since offered to open their own house to little Jane. The great day came when Jane was asked: 'Would you like to come home with us and be our daughter? You can have your own bedroom, your own things.' Bewildered, Jane asked: 'But what have I to do for all this?' 'Nothing at all,' came the reply. 'Only accept us and love us and be our child.' That is what is meant by 'the spirit of adoption'. We are being called now to give a good reception to the love of God in Jesus Christ and simply to acknowledge that we are his children. 'As many as received him, to them gave he the right to become the sons of God.'

So there is our listening, God's offering, and our receiving. But the text names one thing more: becoming. Are you becoming? 'Becoming one of the sons of God' – what does that mean? Surely we are all God's children, everybody is? We recognize that every time we pray 'Our Father'. But according to Archbishop William Temple, the New Testament writers referred to the children of God as those enabled in some measure to reproduce the character of God. The Christian gospel speaks of two kinds of son. There is the son who uses his home and all that it has to offer, giving very little in return: the son who ultimately with no bond of love or gratitude or desire for much further relationship leaves his father. Then there is the son who all his life realizes something of what his father has done for him. As the years pass the relationship grows deeper. Both are sons of creation, but not by grace. Both are born sons, but the second has become a son too, by his recognizing and accepting the bond of love that his father offers.

If we become aware of God's offering and are in all sincerity ready to receive, we have the right to become somebody, the somebody God wants us to be. That is what the text is saying. He will make us what we can never make ourselves. You cannot live a complete life without giving a good reception to Jesus Christ. The impression is sometimes given that Jesus comes to bring us to our knees. That is partially true, but he comes to do more than just that. It is no less true that Jesus comes to stand us on our feet, to give us a new self-respect.

A man very depressed by his past life had a neighbour who was an artist and had worked for months on a portrait. Eventually the depressed man was invited to see the artist's work. He saw himself on the canvas, yet not himself, for the man in the picture faced the world, head erect, shoulders back, hope and courage in his eyes. 'You think I am that,' he said to the artist. 'You see that in me. Then that I will be.' Jesus 'comes unto his own, and his own receive him not. But as many as receive him to them he gives the right to become the sons of God'. Nothing less than that! Give him a good reception, now.

The Church is a Large Tent

Sermon preached by the Revd Martin Camroux at Immanuel
United Reform Church, Swindon, on 8 September 1996.

*The Revd Martin Camroux, 49, has been minister of Immanuel,
Swindon, since 1991, after serving in Birkenhead and before that
in Southampton. He has been a churchgoer all his life and felt
called from an early age to the ministry, being ordained at 27. He
preaches twice each Sunday, to a congregation of 150 in the morning and 60 in the evening. Each sermon lasts about 25 minutes and
is typed out. Copies are left at the back after the service. Many are
taken by worshippers, as was this one, which was sent in by two
members of the congregation. Mr Camroux spends 12 hours a week
preparing his sermons, beginning as soon as he arrives home after his
last Sunday service. 'It is like painting the Forth Bridge,' he says. 'If
it works, preaching is wonderful. If the sermon does not work, the
service doesn't either. Then it is terrible and by the end of the sermon, I wish I was anywhere but in church. There is a silence in the
church when people are listening, when they are not shuffling their
feet. Worship in the URC centres on the sermon. In that sense, the
sermon for us is sacramental.'*

Texts: Galatians 3.37
Bible: New English Bible

Any of you who share my fascination with American politics
may have noticed that one of the soundbites of the
Republican convention the other week was The Republican
Party is a large tent.' By which they meant the Republican Party
has room for every kind of person and for people of different
opinions.

This idea of the large tent has biblical roots. In the early years, the place of worship in Israel was always a large tent. When you read of them worshipping in 'the tabernacle', the word literally means tent. So when you find a church called the tabernacle, that literally means the tent. The Baptist Tabernacle in Swindon literally meant the Baptist tent. Then too in the Bible you can find the idea of the big tent. Isaiah tells Israel: 'Enlarge the space of your dwelling, extend the curtains of your tent to the full' (54.2). So with all this in mind, I want to take this idea of the large tent and apply it to the Church.

First, the Church is a large tent in that it has room for the whole human family. You can divide up the human race in all sorts of ways. Young and old, male and female, white and black, English, Scots, Welsh, Irish, Swindonian, and non-Swindonian. There is room for all in the Church.

This was one of the questions the Early Church had to decide on almost immediately. Jesus was a Jew. The first Church was Jewish. Very well then, was the Church for Jewish people only or was it equally for all? The answer to that was soon clearly put. Says Paul: 'There is no such thing as Greek or Jew, slave and free-man, male and female, for you are all one in Jesus Christ.'

So every kind of human being finds their place equally within the Church. In a world which is divided there is something inspiring about this inclusive nature of the Church. This is a place where the barriers come down. As James Montgomery put it: 'Life's poor distinctions vanish here . . . Our Saviour and his flock appear, one shepherd and one fold.' This is a challenging commitment to live up to. On one occasion, Gandhi went to a church in South Africa. And they looked at the colour of his skin. And they said: 'Oh no, not for you. There's a church for people of your colour down the road.' In this country, too, black people have not always been welcomed in white churches. Racially, being a tent for all races is a challenge to live up to.

But this isn't the only way in which we limit inclusiveness of the Church. I grew up in small-town Norfolk. In those days, Norfolk people were not really sure what they thought about for-eigners. By foreigners I mean people from Suffolk. We used to think people from Ipswich were more or less beyond the pale. When incomers moved into Norfolk towns, they were not always welcomed in the churches. As someone said to me: 'They come here and we don't know them.'

And then the Church is to be for all ages. And often it isn't. I

was once a member of a church where every now and then everyone got very excited about our young people. Usually, it was
when there was a complaint about what the youth group had
broken. Otherwise I don't remember us discussing young people's work at all. Today, they've got what they want, there's no
damage done any more to the hall. There are no young people
there to damage it. In fact, the hall has been let out now because
they no longer have any use for it.

It's fine to say in principle that children are a vital part of the
Church of today. The real question, however, is are we the kind
of Church which young people can feel they belong to? Does the
Church value the contribution that young people can make? For
example, we often talk about teaching the children, but they
have a teaching ministry as well. It's been a profound experience
for me being a parent. The questions and comments children
make sometimes have a directness and a freshness which is profound. I was explaining to my children the other day about
nuclear weapons. Michael said to me: 'Daddy, why don't governments get rid of them?' Ah, Michael, that's a question, isn't it! Or
there was the question my daughter Eleanor asked me recently:
'Why do we call God, he. He's not a boy, is he?' These apparently innocent questions of children are more profound and
more searching than most questions adults ask. The Church is to
be a tent for all the human family.

Second, it's a large tent also in that it is a place where there
needs to be room for diversity of opinion and belief. Some time
ago a woman became a member of one of our churches.
Afterwards she came up to the minister and said: 'Now I've
become a member of the Church, can you tell me what I believe?'
The only answer to that question is: 'No, only you can say what
you believe.' But I suppose she thought the Church was a place
which had a party line. I expect there are churches where that is
true. Ronald Ferguson tells how he grew up in a fundamentalist
church in Scotland. He was given a folding chart. On it were
listed the great controversial questions in religion and what each
of the different churches believed about them. And then was listed
what his church believed – that column was headed 'The Truth'.
That church did have a party line – and all had to stay within it.
Well, in the United Reformed Church, the party line is that there
is no party line. The Church is a big tent. It is a place where there
is room for individual conscience and commitment.

I think there are two fundamentals to which one must hold. First, faith must be centred on Jesus Christ. Then, second, our belief must be based on an honest interpretation of scripture. But granted those two things are in place, the Church is a big tent. There is no party line or one way of thinking. Instead, there is the challenge to work out one's own personal faith according to one's own conscience. And to have the grace to accept others even though they take a different view.

Then, third, the Church is a large tent in that it is a place where nothing we have done means we cannot belong. One of the great controversies of the life of Jesus was between him and the Pharisees. It centred upon what attitude to take to those who had broken the moral and religious law. The Pharisees were happy to welcome them into the life of Israel, but only once they had repented. The Church was for the holy. Others must keep clear.

Jesus did not wait for them to repent. He went among them, caring for them, loving them, accepting them, just as they were. And the Pharisees were horribly shocked. 'Why do you eat and drink with tax gatherers and sinners?' It shocked them to the core. This was the great offence of Jesus in their eyes. This is the background to that story in the house of Simon the Pharisee. There is a woman here who has lived an immoral life. The Pharisees reject her, ostracize her. And she has come to feel a deep sense of rejection. She feels worthless. Without value.

It's a frame of mind we can understand perhaps. In one of the Charlie Brown cartoons, Charlie is talking to his friend, Linus, about the pervasive sense of inadequacy he feels all the time. 'You see, Linus,' Charlie moans, 'it goes all the way back to the beginning. The moment I was born and set foot on the stage of life, they took one look at me and said "not right for the part".' Another time, Charlie complains to Linus about his publisher. 'The publisher sent me a rejection slip,' laments Charlie. 'So what', says Linus, 'lots of writers get rejection slips.' 'Yes,' says Charlie, 'but I didn't send in a manuscript.'

How many people, I wonder, see themselves in that sort of way? The woman in Simon's house certainly did. What she did didn't matter, because she didn't matter – there was nothing going for her. Why pretend there was? When she comes to Jesus, the Pharisees say: 'Can't he see what kind of woman she is?' And then Christ showed her who and what she really was. She was

31

loved, wanted, and accepted by God. Instead of a rejection slip from life, she had an invitation from its Creator. Do you see why she broke down and cried? Christ gave her back her self-respect; showed her she was more than she knew. And she reached up to life and took it.

The Church is to be a large tent, a place where no one is turned away because of what they have been or done. This is good news for all of us. Are there not moments in most of our lives when we too feel isolated, rejected, or of little value? In those moments, it may be hard to believe that God could really love and accept us. For Jesus, however, no one is beyond God's love.

The Church is a large tent. It is a place for all the human family. A place in which there is room for divergence of belief and conviction. A place where nothing we are or have done excludes us from belonging. The gospel call is to make the tent as large as possible – as wide as the love of God.

Sermon for Easter Sunday

Sermon preached by Sally Chapman at Furzebank Worship Centre, Willenhall, West Midlands, on Easter Sunday, 30 March 1997.

The Revd Sally Chapman, 42, is team vicar in the Short Heath team ministry in Willenhall, which at the time of writing was without a rector. The parish has advertised nationally three times for a new rector, without a single applicant in 12 months. Mrs Chapman, whose husband Robert lectures at Dudley College of Technology, has been acting rector by default, but cannot apply for the position herself because the main church of the three in the group does not accept the priestly ministry of women. When she presides there, one-third of the congregation stays away, although they all turn up to hear her preach. Before being ordained, she worked as a science teacher. She started thinking about becoming a priest when she was 6 years old. 'I wanted to be a missionary,' she says. 'The call as an adult came when I had my children. That was when I became more involved in church life. I joined the Mothers' Union and was elected to the parochial church council.' She preaches two or three times a month. 'I look at the passage in the lectionary and carry it around with me for a week or more. I try to pick up on things that are current and relate to them. I might look it up in a commentary.' She writes out her sermons by hand, and tries to keep them within ten minutes. If she has more to say, she saves it for another week. 'I like the opportunity to share part of my own experience and what I feel the church is experiencing, then relating that to our experience as a community. But in some ways I find preaching a trauma. It is quite frightening. It sounds a bit pious, but in a sense the preacher is acting as God's mouthpiece. The day I stopped feeling frightened would perhaps be the day I became blasé.'

Texts: Exodus 14.15–22; Matthew 28.1–10

Bible: New English Bible

A ction! Action by God on behalf of his people is the key theme in both of the dramatic accounts read to us from scripture this morning. Action initiated by God and almost reluctantly taken up by humanity, particularly in that wonderfully graphic story in Exodus. Imagine the scene, the encampment of the Israelites on the verge of freedom, a rather rag-bag collection of all sorts, with whatever they could carry rapidly away with them after their hurried Passover. Scurrying, whole families out of captivity, taking with them their unleavened dough, cattle in herds and all the gold which they had accumulated from the terrified Egyptians in the last days of captivity.

Imagine the clamour, the chaos, which make our Sunday mornings seem organized! Also the fear. Imagine yourself with your children or your loved ones there. Now they are faced with a seemingly impossible barrier, the sea on one side, water representing danger and from behind the pursuit of Pharaoh with his chariots and warriors. Haven't we recently seen such scenes on our television screens in Albania, with whole families seeking to cross the sea to freedom in Italy, being harassed and violated by gunmen out of control, an all too vivid reminder of the dangers of power out of control. Such was the scene facing the Israelites. No wonder their faith was shaken and they cried out to God in anger.

But God, ever present, acts through his chosen agent, Moses. The staff is outstretched and the seas part, and we have that wonderful imagery: 'The waters were torn apart, and the Israelites went through the sea. God had heard the cries of his people, oppressed, beaten, enslaved. Such things are not tolerable to God and so he acts, to bring down the powerful, to dethrone those who abuse the weak.'

This is no pretty story, Charlton Heston movie or not. This story cannot be trivialized. It has been a source of inspiration to oppressed peoples through time. It formed the basis of Afro-American Spirituals during the time of slavery: 'Go down Moses deep down in Egypt's land: Tell old Pharaoh, let my people go.' More recently, it has proved an inspiration to the anti-apartheid movement in South Africa, where liberation has come in our own time. Still it empowers those who in worldly terms seem to have no power, no hope.

The people of Israel, man, woman and child, waited at the edge of the Red Sea in fear, with no hope. Yet the waters were torn apart and the people passed through to freedom. This is a story of faith and hope, of fear and courage, of faithful human endeavour.

Deep waters seem to entrap and to overpower many in our world still. The deep waters of debt. On a small scale we are working towards setting up the Credit Union to release the grip of those caught by the 'divvy-man' and his moneylenders. On a global scale the burden of debt to the international banks, funded by the rich and powerful western nations, has engulfed two-thirds of our world, keeping them in abject poverty, paying back in interest more each year than they receive in aid. These are deep waters which trap hundreds of homeless on our streets. For without a fixed address there is no benefit, no vote, no job, no hope.

The Churches are called to be the Moses of today. We must raise the staff of protest and action on their behalf. We must begin to part the waters of despair. Hold that image in your minds as we focus now on the gospel reading. Here we see another impossible situation, the women coming to the tomb 'to look at the grave'. The imagery used to introduce God's activity is again the control of 'natural forces'. The earth itself is shaken, there is a violent earthquake, the creator of the heavens is about to do a new thing which shakes the foundations of all things.

The stone is rolled away; that impossible, immovable barrier, rolled away by God's liberating power. The angel, God's messenger, sits on it glowing with a pure light, and without violence the men of war are overpowered, lying as dead. The women, however, have nothing to fear, and radically are the first to have revealed to them the result of this activity:

He has been raised from the dead and is going on before you into Galilee; there you will see him.

(Matthew 28.6)

The women are commissioned as apostles, sent with the message to the disciples. But yet more wonders take place. Suddenly Jesus is there before them and he himself gives them the commission to:

Go and take word to my brothers that they are to
leave for Galilee. They will see me there.

(Matthew 28.10)

Let's catch our breath a moment as we, who are almost over-
familiar with this scenario, drink in the scene, take on board
what is going on here. Once more God is breaking through.
Before the barrier was the waters of the Red Sea. Here, the barrier was the stone. Both moved aside.

These are not simply two pretty stories. These accounts are the
foundations of our faith. In our Baptism prayer this morning we
remember both as the children enter the journey of faith.

> We thank you that through the waters of the Red Sea,
> you led your people out of slavery to freedom.
> And through the deep waters of death
> you brought your Son, and raised him to life.
> This is the God of Passover
> This is the God of Easter.

We are a resurrection people, followers of the Way who believe
in a God who does not sleep, but acts on behalf of his people,
whom no barrier can stop. Who breaks through into our lives,
who rolls away whatever stone keeps us imprisoned. For whom
even the waters, a most powerful image in Old Testament times,
proved no match.

But what does that mean? It's powerful stuff, and on Easter
Sunday morning, following the intense drama of Holy Week, it
is easy to feel excited. Yet when the chocolate has all gone, the
turkey is eaten, and hot cross buns have disappeared from our
supermarket shelves, at least until next Christmas, what will be
left? What will be changed?

Let us cast our minds back to the Gospel reading to two
important references, first from the angel:

> He is going on before you into Galilee.
> Then from Jesus, himself:
> 'Take word to my brothers, that they are to leave for
> Galilee.
> They will see me there.'

Galilee. Does it have any importance for us? The gospel writer mentions it twice, which suggests it was very significant for listeners. Galilee was a cosmopolitan place, a place where Jesus preached by the sea. A place where all kinds of peoples gathered. It is the place where at the end of Matthew's gospel, Jesus sends his disciples out 'to make disciples of all the nations'. Galilee is not a holy place like Jerusalem. It is an everyday place where all sorts of people gather for all sorts of reasons. It is a sort of microcosm of the world. It could easily be Willenhall, Walsall or Wolverhampton.

This is important because it tells us that not only we who gather here are God's concern, but that all peoples come under his care, that the essential promise of Easter, of God's active presence in our lives, of freedom, of liberation, is for all. It is our job now to lift these words from the texts and live them. Our belief in the God who liberates, for whom nothing provides an impenetrable barrier, must affect our whole lives. It must affect the great things in life, like the way in which we use our vote in a few weeks' time. It must affect the way we treat one another, both our families, friends and unknown people. We may be the agents who are able to separate the waters of despair or roll away the stones which imprison. We have seen and felt this in our lives. Now we can be the agents who reach out to others, whether they come to church or not. It must affect the priorities we set in our lives. It must affect the way we structure our church budget even.

For we are the messengers of liberation today. We are the ones who will meet the Risen Christ on the streets of modern Galilee where he is before us.

Suffering and Brokenness: the Way to Life

Sermon preached by Andrew Clitherow at St Pauls, Scotforth, on Sunday 24 November 1996.

The Revd Andrew Clitherow, 46, vicar of St Paul's, Scotforth, in Lancaster, has been a priest for 18 years. His call to the ministry came dramatically, while he was having a drink in a pub with a friend who had just been turned down by a Church of England selection board. 'I took him out to cheer him up and convince him he had had a fortunate escape and that ordination was a waste of time,' says Andrew. 'During the conversation I had a very powerful spiritual experience.' This involved what he can only describe as a vivid message from God at that moment, suggesting he become a priest. His father, the late Richard Clitherow, had been Bishop of Stafford and although Andrew studied theology at university, and counted himself a Christian, he became a teacher and had no time for the church or its clergy. But after his experience in a pub, he applied for ordination and before long was himself up before a selection board with a group of other hopefuls. Challenged to say why he was there, he responded: 'I don't want to be here, it is the last place I want to be, but I feel I've got to be, and that's how I got here.' His friend, incidentally, was himself accepted later and is now ordained. To prepare a sermon, Andrew sits down, reads a text and meditates on it. 'The most important thing I will do is pray as much as I can. I chew it over and develop it.' He dislikes preaching. 'I find it difficult. I refuse to preach a sermon whose content is largely predictable. I believe that through prayer and meditation, we should allow God to speak to us and give us what it is we are meant to be saying. For each sermon I go through that process, which I find quite stressful. It is like a birth process, and takes about five hours.' He types out a text, although sometimes preaches without notes or text. But he adds: 'Preaching is primarily a spiritual responsibility, and there is something enormously fulfilling about trying to perform that task. The sermon is a particular and unique form of address. Often I am extremely surprised by the reactions I get. I know there is a lobby to do away with the sermon and to encourage people to engage in dialogue and discussion instead. But I believe that in a post-Christian, secular society there is enormous value to be had from people who have dedicated their lives to God standing up to preach, and trying to relate spiritual truths from the Bible to life as it is today.'

Texts: Genesis 32.22–31 (Jacob wrestles with an angel); Mark 5.24b–34 (The woman with the issue of blood)

Bible: New Revised Standard Version

Travelling on the London Underground on my way to attend a meeting I found myself sitting next to a man who, by his appearance and attire together with his plastic bags full of personal items, was obviously homeless. He was asleep and I guessed that as it was November he must have been glad to have found somewhere warm and comfortable to rest for a while. As I looked at him, his unkempt hair, unshaven face and his old coat, it was his feet that caught my attention most of all. His shoes – what there was of them – were torn and in tatters and I could see that his feet were dirty because he was not wearing socks.

Now I don't know about you but if there is one thing I don't like, it is having cold feet. Cold hands, cold face, cold legs I can cope with, but having cold feet I can do without! I felt particularly sorry for this man, therefore, as walking the streets and living rough must be so much more difficult if you have no protection for your feet in the cold and wet of winter.

So I resolved to give him the socks I was wearing. I wouldn't wake him up; I would just take them off and put them in his pocket. Sadly, though, my own self-consciousness got the better of me. As you know, tube trains are not renowned for their relaxed, informal atmosphere and I just could not bring myself to take off my socks and risk the embarrassment of everyone staring at me. And yet I knew deep down what I should do. Unfortunately, by the time the train reached my destination I had procrastinated too long. Standing on the platform I watched the train pull out with the man still asleep and still without any socks to keep his feet warm.

I felt such a hypocrite. I had been such a hypocrite. I had been given the opportunity to care for someone in need, to love my neighbour, and I had failed. I had let the man down and I had let myself down. What is more, I had let God down. I had allowed my own inadequacies prevent me from putting my faith into practice. I felt wretched and I prayed that I should be given a second chance; that if I could meet the man again, I would give him my socks. Yet, while I attended several further meetings of the same committee in London and though I looked constantly for the man with no socks I searched in vain.

This encounter with another person's suffering had a very powerful effect on me and, as you may know already, it is usually when we are made to feel uncomfortable by someone else or ourselves suffer in some way that we are given the greatest opportunities for spiritual growth.

There is a custom among shepherds in Israel that existed at the time of Jesus and is still practised today whereby if a shepherd senses that a young lamb is going to be a congenital stray, forever drifting away from the flock, he does something that at first appears to be very cruel, but which in fact probably saves the life of the lamb. What he does is to take the lamb and deliberately break its leg so that he has to carry it until its leg is healed. By that time, the lamb will have become so attached to the shepherd that it never strays again.

Jacob, about whom we heard in our first reading, spent half his life struggling with God. He fought against God even when he was about to be given the opportunity to start a new and more honest way of life. Consequently, we are told that God symbolically broke Jacob's hip for him so that in future he would need to lean on God for every step he took in his life.

We need not fear unduly the dark times of life when they come, therefore, as they are often caused by the overshadowing hand of God as he seeks to teach us to rely on him, either by humbling us with another's pain or by breaking us in some way. For we are by nature independent and frequently stubborn. We like to get our own way and it is as if God has to break us first before he can remould us. Jesus told us that we have to die to our selfish interests before our lives can bear spiritual fruit. God cannot raise those things that we have not put to death. It is no coincidence, then, that at various times in our lives and often through suffering we are given the opportunity to look at our superficial ways and lack of love so that through a process of reassessment God can give us a greater nobility of spirit.

There is no other way. For a while we can learn about spiritual growth when we are happy and things are going well, but we only really come to experience it when we are forced to face up to suffering either in ourselves or in others. Such experiences usually come in the most unexpected ways and from the least likely of people who themselves have been broken at some time or other.

In our second reading the woman in the crowd who was made well after touching the hem of Jesus' robe must have been broken many times over. She had an incurable illness that made her a social and religious outcast. Yet from this woman who was unclean and untouchable in the eyes of the establishment, people were to learn that God is more concerned with the state of people's hearts and souls than with the trappings and taboos of formal religion.

This brings me back to the man with no socks. The other day the front doorbell rang. Opening the door I saw standing in front of me a man who was homeless and asking for help. Visitors of this kind frequently call at the vicarage and like many others he asked for food and a hot drink which I gave him. Unlike any others before, he then said: 'I hope you don't mind me asking but have you a pair of socks I could have?' Needless to say, I was more than glad to take mine off there and then and give them to him. He was most impressed that I had given him the socks off my feet. Unfortunately I did not have the time to explain that he had done me a far greater favour than the one I had done for him. For my prayer had been answered. I had been given a second chance and from this so-called outcast of society I had been taught a powerful lesson about myself and my faith.

Life, then, is not a fairytale, even for those who live in castles and ride in carriages. Life has the habit of taking away the facade of respectability which we often hide behind, revealing that for most of us the way forward is to be found not so much with celebrating our successes but, if we are honest, with coping with our failures. Suffering and pain, therefore, should not be seen in entirely negative terms. The Christian faith is not some kind of exemption certificate from suffering; it may in fact make life harder in many respects.

But as Christians we do know that when we fall down, God is

there to lift us up. And this is important if we are to learn how to love, for this process of continually dying and rising is the way of holiness. As Rayner Torkington says in his book, *Peter Calvay – Prophet* (Spennithorne, 1987): 'When you stop falling you will be in heaven; when you stop getting up you will be in hell.'

I would like to finish with some words of Thomas Merton, one of the most prominent Christian contemplatives of our time, who died in 1968. He wrote in his book, *Seeds of Contemplation*, that souls were like wax, waiting for a seal. Their destiny was to be softened in this life to receive at death 'the seal of their own degree of likeness to God in Christ'. And this is what it means, among other things, to be judged by Christ. The wax that has melted in God's will can easily receive the stamp of its identity, the truth of what it was meant to be. But the wax that is hard and dry and brittle and without love will not take the seal; for the hard seal descending upon it, grinds it to powder.

Therefore if you spend your life trying to escape from the heat of the fire that is meant to soften and prepare you to become your true self and if you try to keep your distance from melting in the fire – as if your true identity were to be hard wax – the seal will fall upon you and crush you. You will not be able to take your own true name and countenance, and you will be destroyed by the event that was meant to be your fulfilment.

Salt is Good

Sermon preached by Joyce Critchlow at Christ Church, King Sterndale, Derbyshire, on Sunday 4 October 1995.

Dr Joyce Critchlow, who is in her mid-fifties, and holds a PhD in theology, has lived most of her life in an old Derbyshire vicarage. In 53 years she has missed only one Sunday at King Sterndale church. A lay Reader in the Church of England, she assists in the Buxton team ministry, which has six churches. She also preaches in many other churches in the Diocese of Derby, but always finds time to attend a service at King Sterndale as well. A writer, lecturer and translator, she speaks Russian and is learning to speak Mandarin Chinese. She is also a 'sindonologist', or expert on the Turin Shroud, of 20 years standing, majori ng in the properties of pollen grains which bear closer affinity wi th species known from first-century Palestine than from Medieval France. To prepare a sermon, she looks up the lessons for the day and prays about it. 'Sometimes the message comes straight away and jumps out at me. Sometimes it takes a long time,' she says. She usually preaches from notes, but can deliver an off-the-cuff sermon when a preacher does not turn up. 'However much or little you prepare, you are only an instrument in God's hands,' she says. 'The congregation may see me, but they hear him.'

Texts: Luke 14.34–35

> Salt is good; but if the salt has lost its savour, where-with shall it be seasoned? It is neither fit for the land, nor yet for the dunghill; but men cast it out.

Bible: King James

May the words of my mouth, and the meditations of our hearts, be now and always acceptable in Thy sight, O Lord our Strength and our Redeemer. Amen.

This salt saying of Jesus is recorded not only by St Luke – as we heard in our Second Lesson – but also by St Matthew and St Mark. Each evangelist has given it a different slant, or has inherited a different tradition. St Matthew has Jesus telling the disciples that they are the salt of the earth. By extension, we can apply this to ourselves. Both St Matthew and St Luke imply that, once lost, the saltiness of salt cannot be regained. St Mark, usually the more thoroughgoing of the three writers, leaves open the possibility of tasteless salt becoming salty again.

Scholars have covered much theological mileage in debating which of these sayings is the earliest; but the fact remains that in the three years or so of His ministry, Jesus could have used all three sayings in His teaching.

Of the three, St Luke's is the most 'chemical' – not surprising, since we believe he was a doctor by profession. He leaves his readers the choice of applying these chemical properties to themselves – or not.

When I looked up the lectionary theme for today, and found it was 'The Proof of Faith', I immediately thought: What a contradiction in terms! How does one prove faith? Surely one of the most tantalizing verses of the Bible is in the Letter to the Hebrews, where the writer says: 'Faith is the substance of things hoped for, the evidence of things not seen.'

'The Proof of Faith'. Yes, a contradiction in terms, maybe. But perhaps the disciples of Jesus had much the same problem when faced with His teaching on salt which has lost its saltiness. After all, salt is salty – it isn't tasteless. Or, can it be, or become, tasteless? The short answer is yes. Salt can be tasteless, and it can become tasteless. And in first-century Judaea it could be tasteless to the point of being dangerously poisonous.

What's more, in several ways it could be – and still is – thrown out and trodden underfoot of men (as St Matthew's version has it). When Jesus taught that tasteless salt is worthless, His immediate disciples (and now their twentieth-century descendants) were implicitly invited to interpret His words in a variety of ways. And, as time went on, new illustrations would come to birth. The Dead Sea is noted not only for its high percentage of 'salty' salt, which has for long been commercially extracted, but also, along its coastline, for a range of coloured mineral deposits which today still have an aesthetic commercial value. Among these deposits are white crystals, which look and feel like salt, but have no salty flavour. They are crystals of carnallite – the hydrated chloride of potassium and magnesium – with a bitter, unsavoury taste: salt, which is not salty. From very early times, carnallite was used by unscrupulous traders to make their true salt go further. This is, literally, 'watered down' salt, where the true salt, although crystallising out ahead of the carnallite, has been allowed to be outweighed by the carnallite. It still looks like salt, but has little or no salty taste. Such swamping of Christian saltiness can be seen in the case of religious persecution or harassment overcoming a believer and causing his or her faith to waver or even succumb.

Today, there are still carnallite-type people. They pretend to have faith; they may look and sound like true Christians. But when tested their lack of saltiness shows up and we see them for what they are – pretenders. The danger is that they sometimes do an awful lot of damage before their cover is blown.

Then there was salt which was salty, but of poor quality. This was imported into Palestine from the vast marshes near Larnaca, on Cyprus. It was stored in houses rented for that purpose; but these houses nearly always had primitive, beaten earth floors. Little by little, the salt nearest the ground was spoilt, until the only course was to throw it out into the streets, where passers-by trampled it underfoot. People like this rotten salt are those who don't take their faith seriously. Gradually other interests take over and their faith is not of a sufficiently high calibre to withstand the onslaught. Less and less time is kept for God – until, one day, the world and its glitz have all but trampled their faith into obscurity.

In parts of the Holy Land today, as in the time of Jesus, salt is spread on the flat house roofs. This thickens the roof, which then keeps the house cooler in summer and warmer in winter; it also keeps the roof waterproof in the rainy season since, when mixed in a sufficiently concentrated amount, salt hardens a soil. Since the flat roofs are used for social gatherings, such salt is, like the Larnaca salt, being 'trodden underfoot', but this roofing salt is better salt. It starts life as salt of quality and is put to a useful purpose – but a purpose which seems to fall short of its value as a condiment. Christians like this salt may have great gifts, but use them humbly in the service of others. They play a steady unobtrusive role in the community – often being so much taken for granted as, metaphorically, being trampled underfoot.

Arab bakers on occasion strew the floors of their ovens with salt – sometimes in powder form, sometimes roughly crushed or hammered from large blocks. The catalytic effect on the slow-burning fuel (dried camel dung) increases combustion. After a while, however, the 'combustible energy' of the salt expires and it is then swept up and thrown out into the street – once more to be 'trodden underfoot'. Such Christians play a really vital part in the Church – for a while. Red hot (or perhaps we should say 'white hot') with enthusiasm, they're the life and soul of worship and study group, until their 'combustible energy' flags and, exhausted and burnt out, they retire into virtual oblivion.

Now, let us think of an amount of salt so small that it gives practically no flavour to the food around it. Such ineffectiveness would come from a lukewarm Christian – one determined not to 'rock the boat', or to rub anyone up the wrong way; one capable of influencing no one for good and whose life could be summed up as nondescript, indecisive and pretty useless.

Then consider another type of insipid salt – prevalent in Jesus' time, and not uncommon for seventeen centuries after that. In first-century Palestine, salt was heavily taxed. Dishonest merchants were prone to mix a variety of cheap white powders (often chalk) with the salt, which would then not only be pretty tasteless, but even dangerous to eat – and which had certainly lost most, if not all, of its preserving and aseptic qualities. A Christian with such adulterated salt in his make-up would be one who, while outwardly seeming a Christian, had nevertheless allowed sins and shortcomings into his life. His religion, in other words, would only be skin deep, and liable to crack under pressure.

I've mentioned the differences in the three Gospel accounts of the salt saying. But there is a central part which in each account is common in precept: the riddle 'If the salt has lost its saltiness, how can it become salty again?' The Greek text has several variants of this; so naturally we get an increased number of different translations. The Russians, for instance, take it to mean: 'If the salt has lost its force, or strength'. The Scots have a pithy rendering: 'If the salt has lost its tang, how can the tang be restored?' Tang is a lovely word!

Now, chemically, the definition of 'salt' is: a body which is very readily capable of undergoing double decomposition. That is, a body which, when brought into contact with another, exchanges some of its elementary constituents for those of the other body. In short, a body which is A1 at surviving, in one form or another. So, there's no getting away from salt. If we wanted to, we could not – and live. From earliest times, we have depended for our survival on salt.

Equally, there is no getting away from the true Gospel of Jesus once it has knocked at a person's heart. It's as persistent and essential as the best and finest salt. It can't be annihilated. It can't be explained away. It hangs on in, despite everything any-body can throw at it. In fact, as we've seen in Russia and China (and in many other countries), it strengthens under persecution. I remember Nikita Khrushchev once boasting that he would have the last Christian in Russia paraded on TV. Khrushchev has been dead a long while – and the Church in Russia not only came through the communist regime, but is growing every day.

Like salt, the Gospel is aseptic, in that it cleanses a body as well as a spirit, from sin and the impurities which sin can bring. Once it is applied, it halts the putrefying action of sin in the human pysche. And, as salt is essential for the simplest meal, so is the Gospel of Christ found in the humblest places. As far as the love of God reaches, so the undying, preservative quality of the Gospel is seen.

Jesus was not speaking in merely figurative terms when He taught that unsalty salt was unfit for the land or the dungheap. Both the enriching of the field soil and the controlling of fer-mentation in the hotbed, would be properties valued in first-century Palestine, no less highly than today in many other lands. Salt does not work by remote control; nor can the Christian Gospel be accepted by proxy. Christians, as salt, are given as life preservers to the world, to arrest the processes of corruption in society, by giving freely of themselves (as Jesus gave freely of Himself), in pointing people to God, to accept Christ as their Redeemer, each one for himself.

In Old Testament days, salt was added symbolically to the Jewish sacrifices, to point to their inherent incorruptibility. So the reality and permanence of a Christian life will be recognized by the fire promised at the Last Day: in the fire, that which is merely wood, hay or stubble will be consumed, while that which is of real worth will be forever preserved.

Also in the Old Testament, we have many instances of treaties and covenants being 'sealed with salt' – friendships were cemented by eating salt at a shared meal. Salt, with its preservative qualities, was a symbol of permanence and faith. So the Christian's word should be his bond, allegiance to Christ: an eternal commitment.

In a wound, salt is aseptic, certainly, but if the wound is deep enough, the salt also stings. Christians worth their salt may hurt the world – may indeed get hurt themselves in the process – but it's a blessed hurt, one which, God has promised, will in the end benefit the wounded.

Salt has no substitute. Its deterioration or adulteration leaves a blank which cannot be filled. So it is with a Christian: in the Book of Life, he fills a gap which cannot be infilled by any other. If he loses his saltiness, there will be an accusing lacuna in that Book of Life. Each of us is a 'one-off', with the responsibility which such exclusiveness brings.

In or around the year 90 AD, the learned Rabbi Yosef ben Chananiah was asked: 'If salt has lost its flavour, how will it be salted?' He answered: 'With the afterbirth of a mule.' 'But a mule,' protested the questioner, 'is barren, and can, therefore, have no afterbirth!' 'Neither can salt lose its flavour', came the quiet reply. In the rabbinic view, Israel, the chosen race, was incapable of becoming unsalty salt.

As Christians, we dare not presume to such over-confidence, though at times perhaps our lives do reflect the standpoint of Rabbi Yosef. But in the stillness of our communion with God this week, can we not ask: What is the percentage of saltiness in our spiritual make-up? What proof do we give, or seek to give, of our faith? In short, what kind of salt are we – in our own eyes, in the eyes of the world – and in the eyes of God?

In the name of the Father, and of the Son, and of the Holy Ghost. Amen.

Sermon for the
Fifth Sunday before Christmas

Sermon preached by Roger Dawson at All Saints, East Tuddenham near Dereham, Norfolk, on Sunday 24 November 1996.

The Revd Roger Dawson, 58, was ordained at the age of 26, after working in the publishing industry. His parents were occasional churchgoers and as a boy he was sent to Methodist Sunday school, and then joined the choir in the local parish church. By this time, he was attending church three times each Sunday. At the age of 12, when at grammar school, he heard a sermon by a visiting preacher on 'the call to the ministry'. Roger went to see him afterwards, and said he thought he was called. 'He stood there and laughed his head off,' he recalls. 'He said he was not talking to me. I felt about half-an-inch high and dared not say anything to anyone for years. The signs of being called kept coming back, but it was not until my early twenties that I dared mention it to anyone again.' He went to Salisbury Theological College, was made a deacon at Croydon and priested at Canterbury Cathedral by the then Archbishop, Michael Ramsey. After a row with a bishop, he returned to publishing and worked in the advertising department of Punch, *and then bought a hotel in Cornwall which he ran for five years. When he had had enough of that, he wrote to Ramsey, who sent him to see a friend in Liverpool. He was offered a job in the Church again, at Newton-le-Willows, a small industrial town in Merseyside. He was there for five years as vicar, then went to the British Council of Churches for five years. When the Council was wound up, he went to Covent Garden and ran a hi-fi shop which turned over £1 million a year. He is now rector of Hockering in Norfolk, with four medieval churches with congregations of between 6 and 48. He preaches between two and four times a week. He likes to spend a week preparing his sermons, reading around the themes. He sits down on*

Friday mornings to write them out by hand. 'I like the acting involved in preaching,' he says. 'A Welshman told me once that there were no good Welsh actors until the church stopped recruiting them. I like playing the part, and working the audience, trying to get a response and have a rapport with them, to try and make them listen and give them things they find interesting.' Like others, he entered for the award 'by accident'. He had seen an advertisement in his diocesan newsletter, but thought nothing of it until he knocked over a pile of his old sermons in the kitchen. As he tidied them he started to read them, and was, to his surprise, impressed by one or two. This inspired him to send one in. 'Preaching is undervalued,' he says. 'In some ways, I think the spoken word can be of more value than the written word.'

Two smiling Jehovah's Witnesses knocked on my door the other week. What energy they have for what they believe in. What courage they have for going out and knocking on doors knowing that many will despise them for what they do. 'Did you know', they said to me, 'that the end of the world is near?' My mind flipped to one of my most favourite cartoons – a sandwich-board man whose message is 'The end of the world is nigh' on one side and 'Better pensions for prophets of doom' on the other. The recollection made me laugh. 'I have read your literature', I said, 'and there it says the world was due to end in 1914.' 'Ah,' they nodded wisely, 'that is what we thought then. Now we know that it was not the end, it was the beginning of the end!' 'We are being prepared for the end.'

Today celebrates the beginning of the preparation, not for an end but for a new beginning. I much prefer to work towards new beginnings. Let us take a positive line and not look for endings so much as 'new beginnings'. Our faith should be indicating that our old ways are coming to an end, but only because we are to prepare for the coming of the Messiah, the Christ, the one anointed and appointed by God. It is an attempt to rationalize what actually happens with what we want to happen or what we expect to happen. In Christ all things are made new.

Certainly we know that God used Israel as the people of preparation. If God is to reveal himself to the world it is of immense interest to us to know how he will do it. If he is to use humanity, which nation or peoples will he choose and how will it be effected in history? Looking back with hindsight even the foolish can be wise and we see clearly that God was in dialogue with the people of Israel and he brought them to the point where they looked forward to receiving this Messiah, this person anointed by God himself. But when Jesus did arrive hardly anyone recognized him as the Messiah, which is a puzzle to many of us.

Is it enough to quote the Old Testament and say 'He came to his own but his own received him not' or was he not the Messiah, or was the preparation incomplete, or the people rebellious? I am reminded of a wedding I once took. The bride was only young, just 20, but she had come to me three years before saying she wanted to get married. Her parents would have nothing to do with it until she was 21 and relented a year early only because of enormous pressure. The girl had dedicated her life to getting married, setting up a home. Her whole life was obsessed in becoming a married person. To give them their due the parents worked hard to prepare her for the state of marriage. They paid for both cookery and dressmaking classes at the local college. Her elder sister, married five years before, had a baby and she was a frequent visitor offering advice about childcare and being a mother. When all the reasons why the marriage should not take place seemed to run out, when the preparations, as far as her parents were concerned, appeared to be all complete, a date was set. Preparation turned into run-up to 'the great day'.

The great day arrived and there was so much joyous emotion in the church that I can feel it now as I speak to you. All that hard work, all that looking forward, all that preparation, all that talking, negotiating, cajoling, begging, debating, had drawn the two families together and they stood there before God to mark the beginning of a new relationship. One hour later the girl sat on a chair in the vestry staring at the blank space in the marriage register and asked if we had had the service or did we sign the books before we started. I did not know if it was a joke or not. Many think the service passes so quickly they want to do it again. I asked her if it would make a difference if it were before or after. 'If we have not had the service,' she said, 'I do not want to sign.' But without any prompting she did sign and stood back with a dazed look that everyone said was 'just emotion'.

Israel also could not bring itself to face a new covenant with God. The preparation for them also had become, in itself, a way of life so that they could not bear to see it fulfilled. The process of waiting had been established so firmly that no one could recognize when the waiting was over. Waiting was not a new phenomenon to the Jewish nation. The cream of their society had been exiled to Babylon at one point. 'Just wait till we return', they said. Then they did return but life went on very much as it had before. They complained that they were slaves as they had always been and 'pagan' empires dominated them as so often they had in the past. This could mean only one thing – God was punishing them! So the prophets came out to tell the people to return to Zion. The great restoration had turned out to be a physical event rather than the spiritual return to the promised new life.

It was into this tradition of prophets that another prophet came to the people. A man who led an ascetic life in the wilderness. His name was John and he marked his ministry with baptism. His message was to encourage a return to the spiritual life so that God could visit and redeem his people. Another John, the writer of the fourth gospel, quoting Isaiah, called him the 'forerunner', the one who prepares the way. Israel was seen as the ground, John the plough that prepared the ground in order that the Messiah could grow and flourish. Out of curiosity and need people came to look at the ground newly tilled by John and watered with the waters of the baptism of repentance.

In some excitement there were those who saw a plant growing in the fresh soil. 'It is an undesirable weed', said others who saw new plants as new danger and they quickly pulled it up to destroy it. Only a tiny minority of people recognized it as being a truly new species. Once it had been pulled up from the earth it lasted only a short while in the hands of those who cared for the new plant but the memory of it had an impact upon their lives that would last for ever.

These were the people who recognized that the real return had happened, the exile was finally over. It had happened in and through their Lord, Jesus the Nazarene, Jesus Bar Joseph, the very earthly man whose life now had divine connotations. The cross and the resurrection had not been on their agenda. They recovered only slowly from the shock and horror of it all, but they did begin to see the Kingdom message and the events they had witnessed as the fulfilment of the return from exile promises. Israel's sin had at last been forgiven. God had truly returned to his people. That earlier prophet, Isaiah, had said there would be a remnant and here they were – calling themselves Christians.

If you are saying to yourselves, 'Why did not the rest get the message?' the answer lies in the preparation. When the preparation becomes more important than what the preparation is preparing us for – we are heading for failure. Remember the wedding which for me is so like the nation of Israel? The marriage turned out to be stormy and difficult and the families interfered and bickered. Married life is not the same as the months leading up to it. In six months the girl crossed the road in front of a bus and was killed. No one knows if it was an accident or not. Had she lived it is difficult to see how the marriage would have survived. As Judas discovered, the reality of the day was hard to bear, the arrival infinitely more painful than the walk which preceded it. The people over whom Jesus had wept continued in their old ways, unable to make a new beginning, and the pagan nation that ruled them finally lost patience and destroyed them.

So we shall arrive at Christmas Day and I predict that people all over Britain will be saying what an anticlimax. They will be right of course when the making of mince pies and the shopping is the event, because on Christmas Day that work is completed and comes to an end. However, if our preparation is to prepare for Christ to be with us from that time on it will be a new beginning not an ending.

You and I are a special task force. We are the ones who, thanks to the prophets and saints before us, have recognized God's plan which enables us to go out into His world to announce the message, 'You are my people.' Thus we can rescue those for whom Christmas Day has become an anticlimax. We can turn their endings into new beginnings and Christ will have come on earth to reign.

The Lord's Prayer

Sermon preached by Richard Dormandy at Holy Trinity Church, Sydenham, South-East London, on Sunday 15 September 1996.

The Revd Richard Dormandy, 37, was ordained in 1989 at the age of 29 and he is now vicar of Holy Trinity, Sydenham, South-East London. His parish consists of just the one church, with a congregation of about 75 showing up for the morning service, and a smaller number turning out in the evening. In between London University and Ridley Hall Theological College in Cambridge, Richard sold carpets and worked in a local library. He was converted at 17, after going to church with a youth group he was attending. 'One night, someone explained how to become a Christian. I prayed about it on the tube on the way home. I was converted at that point, as I was sitting down, praying, on the Northern Line.' He adds: 'I told the chap sitting next to me what had happened. He was a complete stranger, and completely bemused.' Richard, whose wife Ruth trained as a counsellor, preaches most Sunday mornings, and in the evenings will either preach a different sermon or do Bible study with the congregation. 'Sometimes I use the lectionary, but I will usually work out a series over several weeks. Each sermon takes a good day to prepare, but I will often be thinking about it for weeks in advance.' He types out his sermons, and occasionally members of the congregation will ask to take them home for private study. He freely admits to revelling in the experience of preaching, 'the telling, explaining, unveiling'. He says: 'I am very at ease, up front, with the performance aspect.' This is partly due to his experience as a singer and songwriter, and he will sometimes accompany parts of a service himself on his acoustic guitar. If he finds himself preaching a duff sermon, he apologizes there and then. 'Preaching can be such a thrilling experience and even the duff sermons can be used quite powerfully by the Holy Spirit,' he says.

The Lord's Prayer

Texts: Psalm 104.1–24; John 1.1–14

Hallowed be your Name

Bible: Good News

The second phrase of the Lord's Prayer has known many mutations. In St Michael-le-Belfrey Church in York you can see the prayer is written on the wall. The artist obviously had to fit all the text into a block that was too small and at the end of the lines some words simply got chopped in half with the result that the prayer now seems to begin 'Our Father which art in heaven, Hallo'. Another mutation is well known, from the child who thought she had discovered God's great secret: 'Our Father in heaven, Harold be your name!' I suppose it's not surprising that children should come out with such ideas – after all, 'hallowed' is hardly a word we use everyday. What does it mean? Well, it means to treat something as holy, to recognize that someone or something is sacred, to decide not to desecrate them. But what does that mean and what does it mean in relation to a name – 'Hallowed be your Name'?

Well you could take a sort of magical view – that the name of God, the word itself should be seen as special in itself, powerful perhaps. 'Hallowed be your Name' in this sense would mean, perhaps, that people should draw back at the mere sight or sound of God's name. But the faith of the Bible has never been a faith based on magic or superstition, and so 'Hallowed be your Name' must go beyond the word itself to the person to whom that name belongs.

All names have meanings and associations – the more unique or famous the name, the clearer the associations. If I say, 'The name's Bond – James Bond', you know exactly what sort of person I am talking about. If my son comes home and says, 'I did a Beckham at school today', then I know it means he scored a goal with a very long-distance lob. A recent magazine advert showed the top half of a man standing in the street. The text read, 'Calvin Klein Jeans'. The implication was that you all know how good our shirts are that you don't need to see the jeans. If I told you I drove a Ferrari it would mean something very different to you than if I said I drove a Volvo, or a Skoda. It would mean I was lying, for a start! Skoda is an interesting case in point, of course, because since they've been taken over by Volkswagen they've actually become a much more sophisticated and – wait for it – 'reliable' car.

In the case of religion, if I talk about 'God' it could mean anything. But when I give that God a name, such as 'Yahweh' or the 'Lord' or 'Jesus', then you can know who I am talking about. The Old and New Testaments are full of revelation about what sort of a person Yahweh is: faithful, gracious, powerful, compassionate, loving, just, true, and so on – his name has a great deal of meaning. What happens if I misuse that name? What happens if I do evil in the name of Jesus? Clearly, the name begins to lose its meaning and people get confused when they hear it. Not only that, but Jesus himself is offended – his reputation is being spoiled.

Let's go back to the idea of a name as a trademark. Suppose Skoda brought out a new model called the Skoda Testarossa. They would probably be sued by Ferrari. Or suppose Sainsbury's started packaging all their products in an identical style to Harrods – they would be taken to court, just as they were by Coca-Cola after which they had to alter the design of their new Classic Cola cans. These are cases of companies saying our name is sacred. You can't apply it to some inferior product or it will lose its meaning and be brought into dishonour.

The ultimate example, I suppose, is that of the artist's signature. 'Vincent' painted into a jug of flowers; 'Renoir' in the bottom left or right corner. The forging of great masters can be very lucrative because their name means so much. I'm always reminded, in this connection, of an episode of *Minder* in which Terry McCann, left alone in the forger's studio, paints a digital watch into a fake Stubbs. It's only after the painting is passed off and sold as original that the anachronism is triumphantly pointed out.

So 'Hallowed be your Name' is perhaps as much about what we should 'not do' as what we should 'do'. When we pray 'Hallowed be your Name' we are praying that God's name should not be brought into disrepute, it should not be attached to things that are not of God. So it might be helpful then, to consider some ways in which the Lord's name is desecrated, so that we can understand more fully why and how it must be hallowed.

A helpful way in is to ask where we see God's signature. And that brings me, at long last, to our readings, because Psalm 104 clearly sees God's signature spread right across the whole world, and John 1 describes how that same signature is printed in a special way upon the church.

Psalm 104 is a magnificent poem, simply describing the beauty and order of creation, and the point is that the beauty and order found there obviously reflect the beauty and faithfulness of God. The wonders spoken of bear his name, and rightly so, for he made them. But God's signature on the world can also be brought into disrepute. People can see it fixed on to things that actually he did not create: starvation, war, injustice, poverty, greed.

The psalmist wants to say, 'Look at this wonderful world which the Lord has made!' But some people would argue, 'It does not seem to me that he made a good job of it – look at all these children being abused by paedophiles; look at all these starving refugees; listen to all these people whose daily conclusion is no more than "life's a bitch and that's all there is to it".' So God's signature is on the world, but it's being desecrated, or brought into disrepute, by things that are not according to his plan.

John Chapter 1 talks about the Word of God becoming flesh – being incarnate in the person of Jesus – and Jesus giving authority to his followers to share in his sonship. The signature of Jesus, the Son of God, is therefore stamped on the Church. We are people who bear his name.

We say, in our hymns and liturgy, 'Look – isn't it great to be in the Church! We have love, joy, peace, community, forgiveness – and all because of Jesus'. But some would argue, 'What is this Jesus like? Look at his Church: it's snobbish, stand-offish, the ministers are power mad; they protect their own at the expense of justice; what about those priests who sexually abuse people and are quietly moved on as if nothing happened? What about the atmosphere or awkwardness that is created if someone dares to disagree with, or question, or doubt the received wisdom or articles of faith? What about people whose experience of the church is not one of liberation but of repression?' And so Jesus' signature on the Church is also brought into disrepute – desecrated by the Church itself.

When we pray 'Hallowed be your Name', we are not talking about the cultural niceties of holiness – the questions of whether you follow this custom or that custom. Neither, when we pray 'Hallowed be your Name', are we talking about the awesome terror of magical holiness -the sort of Indiana Jones and the Temple of Doom idea of holiness. But when we pray 'Hallowed be your Name' we are praying that God's name, his reputation if you like, his identity will be kept pure and unimpeachable. We are praying, therefore, that his world will be characterized by kindness, compassion, truth, transparency in relationships. We are praying that his Church will be a community of grace and righteousness, sacrifice and freedom.

Now, you may say, 'Surely God doesn't need us to guard his reputation – he's not much of a God if he cannot defend himself.' And such a statement would be true: of course God can look after his own name, but he invites us to be involved for two reasons.

First, he invites us because he loves us, and his love is always outwardgoing and inclusive. He wants us to join with him in upholding his cause, and as our Father, he knows it is good for us to join him because it strengthens us morally and spiritually to be committed to the good things that his name represents.

Second, he invites us because to exclude us would be to take away our chance of repentance. When God's name is cleared and hallowed, we, no less than anyone, are the ones left wanting. The Day of Judgement is sometimes referred to in the Bible as the day when God's Name will be upheld by all, but because of his mercy, his long suffering, and his compassion for us, our Father holds off on the vindication of his own name, because such a vindication would implicate us so badly. While he denies himself the opportunity to be vindicated, he offers us the continuing opportunity for repentance. He says, 'I can vindicate myself, but I am held back in order to give you the opportunity of repentance.'

When we pray 'Hallowed be your Name', therefore, we are expressing a longing that our Father's name, and that of his Son, Jesus, will be held in high honour throughout the world. We are also expressing repentance for the parts we've played – however big or small – in the desecration of that name. And finally, we are committing ourselves to the upholding of that good name.

What does this commitment involve? In closing, let me lay before you three tasks. The first is to keep doing the things that reflect the character of our Heavenly Father. Keep living the life of Christ through the Spirit that lives in you. Be truthful, be compassionate, get involved where you see God's purposes for the world and the Church being damaged. Too often we wait for someone else to speak up or for someone else to take the initiative. When business consultants were conducting interviews at the company 3M they were astonished to find that proposals for a new product rarely exceeded five pages. The vice president explained, 'We consider a coherent sentence to be an acceptable first draft for a new product plan.' Jesus said, 'Be perfect as your Father in heaven is perfect' – but too often we hold back, faltering at the first draft stage.

So that is the first task in upholding the good name of our Father – to do his will, to do things that reflect his character. The second task is to keep fighting those things in the world and Church – and in our own lives – that slander God's character.

On Friday I was talking with Enzo from the Merchant of Venice shop in Forest Hill. He told me that when he was 20, he and some friends went to preach the gospel in the poor parts of Palermo, where he comes from. Unfortunately, he said, they noticed just how poor the people were and realized that they had to do something practical to help them, so they set up a local relief charity which has been running for 23 years.

Poverty is like crude graffiti scrawled over the beautiful world our Father has made. The prayer 'Hallowed be your Name' is a commitment to fight it. But praying such a prayer nearly always brings enemies and criticism. Archbishop Helder Camara struggled for the poor of Recife for many decades and made many enemies. He said, 'When I give food to the poor they call me a saint. When I ask why the poor have no food they call me a communist.' When we are called to God's work, we should not hold back through fear of criticism. But perhaps the first enemy is our own inertia: taking the next step towards living the gospel we proclaim.

So those are the first two tasks involved in a commitment to 'Hallowed be your Name' – to do the things that reflect his character and to fight the things that slander his character. These two tasks need to be applied both to the world and to the Church – for there are many things in the Church of Christ that cast a terrible slur on his name, and it should not be so.

The third, and final, task is to declare what God has already done – to remind ourselves and to inform others of how great is his name. Every now and then, one of the London art galleries stages a major exhibition of a famous painter such as Dégas or Cézanne, and these exhibitions remind us of how great those artists' names are. In the same way we need reminding and educating about the character and faithful deeds of God, as revealed in Scripture and in history. We can do it in all sorts of ways – casual conversation, organized mission, church worship, the written word.

This morning we declare the greatness of God's name as we share in the bread and wine. For as we eat and drink these gifts we are reminded graphically of his total commitment to us – such that he gave up the security of the heavenly home, was born as a fragile baby, and gave up his body and blood on the cross. He did it because he is God, and because he lives up to his name of 'Wonderful Counsellor, Prince of Peace, Everlasting Father, Lamb of God'.

Earlier this week a story broke about billions of pounds worth of Nazi gold that had been stored since the end of the war in Swiss bank accounts. Swiss banks are, of course, known for their utter confidentiality, but their government has ordered a full-scale inquiry with unprecedented access to all records. The ITN reporter on Thursday night said, 'For the Swiss it is highly embarrassing and their main priority now is to restore the country's good name.'

When we pray 'Hallowed be your Name' we are praying for something similar – a restoration of our God's good name in the world, that it may be given the honour and acclaim it is due.

Christian Unity

Sermon preached by John Garland at Elfed Avenue United Church, Penarth, Vale of Glamorgan, on Sunday 19 January 1997.

The Revd John Garland, 55, began working life as a secondary school teacher. For 17 years, until 1990, he was head of history at Barry Bishop Comprehensive School in the Vale of Glamorgan, where he has lived all his life. 'I did some lay preaching and this was reasonably well received, and I wondered if someone upstairs was trying to tell me something,' he says. He first became a part-time Baptist minister, and combined that with teaching. But eventually, finding the pressure of modern teaching had become 'ridiculous', he took the chance to transfer to full-time stipendiary ministry, and now heads the Llandough Baptist Church, which has a congregation of about 40. He preaches every Sunday. 'Unlike many Noncomformists, I do believe in the discipline of working to a lectionary,' he says. He uses the one authorized by the Church of England, to keep in touch with 'mainstream Christianity'. He prepares by reading, and devises a snappy sermon title which he allows to gestate for four or five days. He likes to have a text in front of him when he preaches for security, although he rarely reads from it. 'Preaching is a challenge, firstly to capture people's attention, and then when I have it, to relate stories from a 2,000-year-old book to the lives that ordinary, working-class people have today.' When he started, he had to force himself to preach, belonging in that category of 'those rather shy people who find themselves in positions of prominence'. He only entered the award because one of last year's shortlisted preachers twisted his arm. Besides the church, his other love is cricket, and he is a vice-president of Glamorgan County Cricket Club.

Texts: Romans 12.4–5

For just as in a single human body there are many limbs and organs, all with different functions, so we who are united with Christ, though many, form one body, and belong to one another as its limbs and organs.

Bible: Revised English Bible

One of the expressions which passed into the English language as a result of the hippy movement of the 1960s was 'to do your own thing'. It's not perhaps the most elegant of expressions, but surely there's something profoundly Christian about it. It suggests sincerity, tolerance, a desire to be ourselves and show ourselves to others as we really are, without hypocrisy or pretence.

Not many of us have never tried to hide behind an image of some kind, if only for form's sake. And sometimes the image we present at home can be very different from the one we shelter behind in the office or at the club. 'Doing your own thing' is an attempt to do away with all these facades. It says: 'Look, everybody, I'm me, and I refuse to conform to any patterns laid down by others which would make me less than I am. I'm a free human being, proud of my individuality. I refuse to cloak that individuality in anybody else's false image.' That's 'doing your own thing.' And very wise and healthy it is too.

But what about when we come to church? What happens to 'doing our own thing' when we pass through those doors? There's a widespread belief that organized religion is the enemy of individuality and freedom, and we Church people are largely responsible for that belief. So often we give the impression that Church people must conform to a pattern – dress in a certain way, have a shared set of beliefs and value systems – must do the Church's thing rather than our own. Even worse than that, a curious aura of 'churchiness' seems to come over quite normal men and women when they get involved in Church matters. They seem afraid to show their real selves, afraid that 'their own thing' somehow won't be acceptable. So instead they conform to an expected pattern. I do not know how true this perception actually is, but it's widely held out there. And it has led many people both within the Church and outside to be very frightened of the ecumenical movement. If the Anglican has learned to do the Anglican thing, and the Baptist has learned to do the Baptist thing, if the Presbyterian has learned to do the Presbyterian thing, then what on earth would happen if we all came together? Wouldn't we all get submerged in some huge bureaucratic Church, faceless and impersonal, which would expect us to conform to its own special 'thing', so that any last spark of individuality we may possess would finally be snuffed out? What possible room could there be in a united Church like that for the individual to be himself, to 'do his own thing'?

As someone involved in the ecumenical movement here in Wales, I can assure you that our vision of a uniting Church is nothing like that, for the very best of reasons. Look at scripture. Look at Isaiah's vision of the Lord's servant, which surely is what the Church is meant to be: 'He will not break a crushed reed or snuff out a smouldering wick.' Is there anything overbearing or faceless about that? And what about the Early Church which broke down barriers of conformity by baptising Gentiles as well as Jews, and which refused to force Gentile converts to adopt Jewish ways? Above all, how would such an image fit in with a God who created this world of ours to sparkle with the most astounding variety? Think of the incredible differences between species of fish in the seas, birds in the air, beasts in the forest, people of every race and colour. To believe in God's creation is to see a universe tingling with difference, where each throbbing atom, each circling planet, each creature from the ant to the hippopotamus, and each individual human being, is busily 'doing its own thing'.

And what's true of our creation is surely equally true of our redemption. Need every Christian man or woman entering a church give up every trace his individuality? Do those who dedicate their lives to Christ's discipleship get baptised into a standard pattern and automatically cease to be themselves? Here look at the first disciples. Were the blustering Peter, the bashful Andrew, the sceptical Thomas, the militant James and John any less themselves after their call to discipleship? The whole New Testament is crowded with human personalities, each one amazingly different, each one 'doing his own thing'. And so it has been with all the saints through all the ages of the Church's history.

What the gospel offers us is a spiritual grace which meets us just where we are. We're not asked to change ourselves into somebody else. Jesus shocked the religious leaders of his own day precisely because of this. He accepted a huge variety of people, tax gatherers and prostitutes included, just as they were, because he valued them as individuals just as they were. And to this day he does not look for special kinds of people for his Church. God created us in an abundant variety; he has redeemed us with all our originality and difference. So, says Paul in our text, you mustn't think of the Church as a club for the temperamentally religious. Think of it instead as the body of Christ on earth. And what can be more different in shape and size and function than the parts of a body: an ear, an eye, a nose, a leg. Each one, thank God, does its own thing, otherwise we'd soon be in a doctor's hands, or a surgeon's. Each one is a 'member' of the body. Each one of us is a member of Christ's body, the Church. Jesus wants you in his Church, not some imitation you trying to do somebody's or something else's 'thing'.

Well, if that's the whole truth, then what am I, a Baptist minister, doing here in a United Reformed/Presbyterian church this morning? And what is your minister doing standing at my Baptist communion table in Llandough? Shouldn't we just accept the fact that we're all different, and then go our separate ways, doing our own separate things? Why should we bother working and praying for Christian unity? Wouldn't such unity be a denial of the very individuality we all ought to be seeking? The fact is that 'doing our own thing' is not the whole truth, it's only half the story. The other half is this. What about the clash which must inevitably come when me doing my own thing hinders you from yours, or when I, in insisting on my own freedom to be myself, deny you the freedom to be yourself? Aye, there's the rub.

So you see, there has to be a limit to 'doing one's own thing', because if there is not, chaos results. Think back for a moment to the created world with its wonderful variety of life and form. There's a wide variation, but that variation is demonstrated within a fixed and ordered pattern. Freedom without order is chaos, and whatever else it might be, the world of nature is anything but chaotic. Watch David Attenborough and see. An astonishing order permeates the whole creation, and it's that very order which makes the infinite variety possible. Without it, everything would collapse. What's true of nature is true also of human nature. Every human society that has ever appeared in history has evolved its own set of rules. The individual's freedom to do his own thing is circumscribed by those rules. Without them, anarchy would reign, and anarchy, far from expanding freedom, destroys it. Without the discipline of an ordered society, there's just no possibility of doing one's own thing. Think of an orchestra. The trombone player wants to be free to turn in a virtuoso performance. But to do that he must accept the discipline both of the composer's score and the conductor's baton. Without that discipline, chaos would ensue and his would-be freedom be lost to him.

That's what is wrong with a divided Church. Here we are, you in your small corner and me in mine, all busily doing our own things, and all failing totally to calculate the effects of this on our neighbours. The human body only functions properly when the brain directs the activities of the parts. It's the brain which co-ordinates the function of the limbs and organs. It's the brain which makes the legs walk, the arms swing, the eyes see, the ears hear, the nose smell. Take the brain away and there's chaos, the body collapses. For nearly five hundred years the various churches have gone their own separate ways, like discordant limbs and organs of a single body. Is it any wonder that they argued and clashed with one another? Is it any wonder that there have been dozens of Northern Irelands throughout history, and that people outside have been confused or disgusted by all the bickering and infighting? 'All of us form one body,' wrote Paul to the Romans, but the key qualification comes next: 'if we are united with Christ.' Our body functions as one body if we're in tune with the brain which makes the parts function according to a pattern. Christ is the head of the body, the Church is the brain that co-ordinates the activities of its members. And for centuries we in our separate compartments have manifestly not been united with Christ. Is it any wonder, then, that the body has gone berserk?

That's why the ecumenical movement is important. That's why Church unity matters. Not so that I can get my way or you can get yours, but so the both of us and others too can subject ourselves once more to the leadership of Christ, the head, the brain which should be directing all our actions. This very service, in its own small way, is a contribution to that process. Wednesday's press conference in Cardiff, when we release plans for an ecumenical team for east Cardiff led by an ecumenical bishop, will be a huge contribution, if we have the vision to make it come to pass. We live in exciting times, but we've got centuries of ignorance, prejudice and fear to wipe away. We're only just starting along the path to find again the mind of Christ. But if we do find it, and together submit ourselves to it, we needn't fear the uniting Church we're seeking will be faceless and bureaucratic, imposing a dull blanket of uniformity. It's when that day comes, when we're at last prepared to accept the discipline of obedience to Christ, that then and only then will each of us really be free to 'do his own thing'.

'If Any Man Would Come After Me, Let Him Deny Himself'

Sermon preached by Anthony Gledhill at the Central Methodist Church, Kettering, Northants, on Sunday 16 February 1997.

The Revd Anthony Gledhill, 75, has been retired for 10 years but still takes services regularly because of a shortage of preachers in his local Methodist circuit. He entered the ministry in 1946 on leaving the Air Force, where he was a flight engineer in Bomber Command. Theological colleges were full because of the wartime backlog, so he went first to a church and then to Wesley College in Bristol. He spent two years as a missionary in Nigeria and was ordained when he returned in 1951, going on to minister in South Wales, Lincolnshire and Norfolk. A churchgoer all his life, his boyhood heroes were not football or pop stars, but preachers such as Leslie Weatherhead and Eddie Sangster in Leeds where he grew up. He preaches once a fortnight, using a word processor he bought last Christmas. He always starts with a Bible text, and expounds on that. He also tries to use humour and likes to spend up to three weeks preparing a sermon. He prefers not to use a manuscript, feeling that it inhibits his delivery. However, he makes more extensive notes than he used to, to help him stay to the point. 'I find getting older that I tend to ramble off at a tangent,' he says. 'I can get a bit long-winded.' He believes the sermon is a teaching tool. 'I try to answer some of the questions people ask these days,' he says. 'When dreadful things happen, they say: "Where is God?" I centre on the goodness of God, and the reality of sin and evil.' He believes people rarely remember the information delivered in a sermon, but are helped by the experience. 'People are somehow helped by the fact of sharing,' he says.

Texts: Mark 8.34

> If any man would come after me let him deny himself, and take up his cross, and follow me.

Bible: Revised Standard Version

I really must get myself a new bathmat. There's not much wrong with the old one. I put it in the washing machine and it comes up lovely and fluffy. But after a few hours it develops a huge crease down the middle. Something to do with the foam backing I think. It's a bit like me really. I confess my sins, as we did earlier in the service, but I find myself falling into the same weaknesses over and over again. It is comforting to find that St Paul himself had the same problem. He tells the Christians in Rome: 'I have the desire to do what is good, but I cannot carry it out. I find myself doing, not the good I want to do, but the evil I do not want to do.' Who on earth can set me free from the clutches of my own sinful nature? It's rather like those trolleys in the supermarket. You try to push them in one direction, but they want to go in another. What are we to do?

A man was eating his packed lunch at work. 'Oh dear,' he said, as he looked at his sandwiches, which yet again were sardine. 'Well,' said his mate, 'why don't you ask your missus to pack you up something different?' 'That's the trouble,' he replied, 'I make them myself.' The remedy was in his own hands. So it's with ourselves. 'Well, thank you very much, Lord! I turn to you for help, and you tell me it's all up to me.' The season of Lent is about self-denial, doing without this or that as a matter of discipline, denying yourself sugar in your tea, chocolates, cigarettes, or whatever indulgence is appropriate for you. Nothing wrong with that, but I think self-denial goes much deeper. It involves denying ourselves, seeing all the 'creases in the bathmat' and saying firmly, that's not me. If I want to progress in the Christian life, if I want to move on from the old life with all its 'creases', I must begin by denying myself.

The Welsh comedian Max Boyce tells how he was, as a boy, due to recite at an Eisteddfod. It was a poem in Welsh entitled 'The Squirrel'. Max gave out the title and his mind went blank. Try it again said the adjudicator. 'The Squirrel', said Max, but he could not get any further. All his family were in the front row, trying to prompt him by mouthing the words. They looked like a row of goldfish, he says. A lady said to his mother: 'Isn't that your little boy, Mrs Boyce?' 'Never seen him before in my life,' said she. She disowned him. It seems to me that this is what self-denial is about. Denying myself. Disowning myself.

A young lady recently featured on Anglia television had lost several stones in weight, and become a different person. She testified that her determination came when she saw a photograph of herself and said: 'That's not me!' So when I look at myself, and see all the 'creases in the bathmat', I say: 'That's not me.' This is the beginning of progress in the Christian life.

But if that's not me, what is? On holiday one year in Cornwall, we passed a flock of sheep in a field and my daughter remarked: 'Those are proper sheep.' I should explain that we lived in South Wales at the time, in the mining valleys, and the sheep that Elizabeth was used to seeing were the scrawny, half-starved looking sheep which used to invade our gardens from the mountain, looking for sustenance. The Cornish sheep were plump and woolly, just like the ones she had seen in her picture books. They were proper sheep, as sheep were meant to be.

The Protestant reformer, Martin Luther, used to speak of Jesus as 'the proper Man'. We might prefer to say 'the proper human being.' Man, or woman, as God intended that they should be. The good news of the Bible is that God sees us all, not as we are, with all our creases, weaknesses and sin, but as we might be. He invites us, in St Paul's words, to 'put on Christ.' A Christian classic, written by St Thomas à Kempis, is entitled *The Imitation of Christ*. That gives the impression that we have to go about pretending to be Jesus, like an actor playing a part. This is the kind of hypocrisy that Jesus himself was always warning about. He accused the leaders known as Pharisees of parading their piety, putting up a pretence of being better than they really were. But they had never looked at themselves. They were like the person St James tells us about who looks at himself in a mirror and immediately forgets what he looks like. They thought they actually were like the part they were playing.

People sometimes imagine that actors are like the characters they portray in real life. Actors are often asked in interviews whether in real life they are like the characters they portray. Sometimes they will admit that there is something of that character in them, but often they will say: 'Oh no, I'm not really like that at all.' We can only avoid the hypocrisy that Jesus warns us against if we are constantly recognizing and rejecting the self with all its 'creases', and aspire to be the 'proper' person that God knows we have it in us to be.

In an episode of the TV drama series *Colditz*, a prisoner

decided to try and contrive his release from the camp by feigning madness. He did this so convincingly that he achieved his object and was repatriated to the home land. The tragedy was that he had played his part too well and the balance of his mind had tipped. Sadly, he had actually become insane. That was only a story, if a very moving one. But I believe it contains a truth that can help us. If, as we play a part, we are consciously aspiring to be the character we are portraying, we can be transformed into it. If we are genuinely attempting to 'put on Christ', we may by and by be shaped into his image.

The Lenten austerities can help in this. They remind us that, having rejected the temptations of Satan to achieve his kingdom by worldly means, Jesus set his feet on the road that led to the cross. We cannot expect our own way to be any easier. The 'old self' must be crucified. The trials that life brings our way, the darkness through which we sometimes pass, can become a blessing, as James says in his Epistle, if they help us to see ourselves more clearly, and deny what we are, so that we may become our 'proper' selves, in the likeness of Jesus. Many folk find it hard to accept that God loves them, since they are so painfully aware of 'the creases in their bathmat', but they need to remember that God sees us, not as we are, but as we may be, when his grace and the power of his Spirit have transformed us.

St Paul tells us to 'work out our own salvation'. As we have seen, this is cold comfort if that is where it ends. To be told that it's all up to you is not very helpful, if you leave it there. But the Apostle goes on to say 'God is working in you', and that makes all the difference. As we reject the 'old self', God through his Spirit works alongside us to create the new.

As W. Bright's nineteenth-century communion hymn, 'And now, O Father, mindful of the love', puts it:

Look, Father look on His anointed face,
And only look on us as found in him;
Look not on our misusing of Thy grace,
Our prayer so languid, And our faith so dim;
For Lo! between our sins and their reward,
We set the passion of thy Son our Lord.

A Sermon for Remembrance

Sermon preached by Gill Green at St Mary's Church, Hemel Hempstead, on 7 May 1995, the Sunday before VE Day.

Gill Green, 56, is a reader in the Church of England and attends St Peter's, a medieval church at Ousden, near Newmarket, Suffolk. A retired teacher, she used to teach English to children with learning difficulties. She kicked against a strict Christian upbringing with the 'Brethren', and found it difficult to accept their insistence that women should not only be silent in the churches but in prayer groups as well. Like many former Brethren, she eventually found her home in the Anglican church. 'For 15 years I had no faith at all,' she says. 'I went a bit wild once the brakes were lifted off.' She returned to Church after her daughter, who was singing in the local church choir, pleaded with her to join because it needed some altos. 'It was like coming home. I gradually became aware that I always had believed,' she says. 'I had turned my back on something but it never stopped being there. When I turned around and faced it, it was there again. I always thought I needed to walk alongside God. Now I realize that He walks with me.' She preaches every week in one of the four churches in the Benefice. She reads the lectionary on the Monday before, lets it gel and returns to it during the week. By Thursday, she normally has an idea of what she will say. She writes the sermon on a word processor on the Saturday night, spending about four hours getting it down. She might try to include messages of support and help for those in trouble in the community, 'for example, if I have heard there's been a rift somewhere, or if the PCC is having difficulties.' She preaches for 12 minutes. 'It is like telling them something they already know, but putting it in a different light,' she says. 'It is holding something up, and showing how the light shines through. I don't like being in the pulpit, I prefer to be on my feet on the floor, and to walk around a bit.'

Texts: Ezra 3.13

No-one could distinguish the sound of the shouts of joy from the sound of weeping, because the people made so much noise. And the sound was heard far away.

Bible: New International Version

It was still dark when Miriam woke. For a moment she couldn't remember why she had woken so early, then as memory returned she was filled with excitement. Still in her nightclothes, she slipped from her bed and ran silently on bare feet into her brother's room. 'Micah, wake up!' she hissed into his ear. 'It's Temple day!' For once, he did not bury his head into his pillow. Quite as excited as his sister, he thought with eager anticipation of what the day promised.

Later, the two children, holding tightly to their parents' hands, hurried along the empty streets. Although all four had risen before dawn, their preparations had taken longer than they had expected. By the time they left their home in Straight Street, it seemed as if the whole of Jerusalem was deserted. Yet although they saw no one, they could hear in the distance a sound like the murmuring of the sea. It rose and fell, gradually increasing in volume the nearer they came. It was the sound of a great crowd. For a few minutes there was utter silence. Then thousands of voices rose in song. Even the children recognized the melody of one of the great responsorial psalms. Again there was silence, and then, as Miriam struggled to keep up her half-running step alongside her father's long stride, she gradually became aware of a great sense of fear. For the air now throbbed first with the sound of wailing, next with a great shout of triumph. Then quickly the two distinct sounds became one and Miriam could not have said whether she was listening to the deepest grief or to rapturous joy.

That night, as she lay in bed watching her mother tidying the room, Miriam asked. 'Mama, why was that old man crying, the one we shared our dinner with? And I saw lots of other people crying, too. I thought today was supposed to be happy?'

Her mother's busy hands became still and she came across the room to sit on her daughter's bed. 'Listen,' she said, 'today is a happy day and a very special day because the foundation stones of our new temple have been laid. Now at last we shall have a proper place in which to worship God. But lots of people are sad. Some of them, the really old ones, can just remember the Temple as it used to be – King Solomon's Temple. They know that this new one can never be the same – not as big nor as splendid. But more than that, they remember all the things that have happened since that Temple was destroyed in the war. They saw so many people they knew being taken off as prisoners to exile in Babylon. A few of them went there themselves, although of course they were only children at the time. They are weeping for what might have been. Yes, today we are starting again, but the memory of the past can never go away.'

Many years later, another Miriam, one hundred generations on from the first Miriam's line, hesitated at the entrance to Yad Vashem. It was still not too late to change her mind. She could get back onto the coach and re-read her guide to Jerusalem. War was not her thing, and she felt that she knew quite enough about the horrors of the last one. She thought of the sepia photographs of people she had never seen, lovingly stroked by her mother's fingers as she went over the familiar recitation: 'Your Uncle Jakob – he was sent to Auschwitz. That's my cousin Naomi – such a pretty girl. She died in the ghetto in Warsaw. And Reuben – we never did find out what happened to him.'

'Mother would expect me to look round,' thought Miriam, 'so I can tell her what it's like.' And clutching her guidebook, Miriam went into the museum, built to commemorate the six million Jews who died in the Holocaust. Some years later, in 1997 to be precise, Miriam sat at the table, her family beside her. The children had been making plans for the weekend ahead. 'Mum', said the eldest child, 'I know a bit about the war because we've done it in school.

But I don't think we should make anything special out of next Sunday, Remembrance Day, or whatever it's called. I don't want to wear my poppy, either. War's horrible, and the sooner we can forget all about it, the better.' As she looked round the table at her children, Miriam found herself in memory back at Yad Vashem. She remembered how shaken she had felt as she looked at the photographs – the starkness of the black and white high-lighting the contrasting values they portrayed. Hatred versus love. Greed versus self-sacrifice. Self before others. She remembered how, searching for composure, she had left the main museum building and gone into a garden, sunlit, secluded.

There she had found and entered the Children's Memorial. How was she to share with her children, carefully shielded as they were, the unutterable poignancy of that black space, so dark that her feet seemed to be in another world, yet lit by a million stars? Out of that space swam towards her the face of a child, while a voice dispassionately gave the child's name, and the place and date of death. Another picture followed, more details and yet more faces until, unable to cope with the unending litany, she had stumbled, weeping, out into a dazzling day.

Miriam smiled across the table at her child who, God be thanked, had grown up in a freedom which those other children had never known. 'You are quite right,' she said. 'War is horrible and we shouldn't honour it. But we can sit here like this because of very many brave people who lived their lives before we were given our chance to live ours. Lots of them are buried in war graves in rows like troops on parade. Some of them don't even have a cross to mark the place where they died, and those who loved them best can't picture where they are lying. So it's right that we should honour them and remember that we are free today because of what they did. But the very best way to do that is to live in a way that makes very sure that war can never happen again. And that's hard to do because grown ups seem to like fighting.'

'I do too!' said Miriam's youngest. 'But when I'm shot dead I always get up again!'

'Well,' said Miriam, 'wearing your poppies this weekend will remind you that there are lots of people wounded or disabled in the war who will be helped by the money that is raised when they are sold. And though we live in freedom now, it's only because many people were brave enough to fight for us, and to die for us, too. You know, there's a memorial to people who died in the war that says how important it is that we should remember. The words on it are "Remember. Never, never forget. Never allow the lessons of history to die on you. Let every day be a Remembrance day".' And, as quietly, thoughtfully, her children got down from the table, Miriam knew that a lesson had been learned.

As Christians, we have a weekly reminder that death is not the end. When we join together to celebrate the eucharist, we affirm our belief in the heart of the Gospel, that Jesus rose from the dead. Through that most amazing fact, we can believe that God in the end will cancel out evil. What happened to Christ is the evidence. We believe that His resurrection bears witness that the righteous shall be held in everlasting remembrance.

And we can believe that when the end of all things comes, as come it must, there will be no mistaking the sounds of rejoicing for the sound of weeping. For in Christ all will in the end, be harvest. Amen.

Who was John?

Sermon preached by Zena Helliwell at Redland Parish Church,
Bristol, on Sunday 15 December 1996 at 10 am family worship.

*Zena Helliwell, 53, has been a reader in the Church of England for
three years and a churchgoer all her life. She worked in business
until her mid-thirties, when she became a teacher. She is currently
head of religious studies at Clifton High School, Bristol. She is usually given a passage of scripture chosen by the vicar to preach on.
About a week before she is due to deliver it, she sits down, meditates
on the passage and reads around the subject, looking it up in various
commentaries and reference books. She tries to think up illustrations
before writing it down and preaching from a text. The entire process
takes 6 hours, and she preaches for 25 minutes. 'I enjoy being able to
make the Bible text come alive for people, to get it across to them, to
make it live for them, so they can understand what it really means,'
she says. 'I feel preaching builds up the congregation in their
Christian faith. It encourages them to go on.' Outside teaching and
preaching, she is an expert in handicrafts. She does graphic design
work for several charities, including Compass Braille, which she
became interested in because her best friend is blind. She also plays
the piano.*

Texts: John 1.19–35
Bible: New International Version

I'm going to begin by telling you a true story. The year was
1979. The town was Kotor. That's in former Yugoslavia. It was
shortly after 7 o'clock in the morning. The beautiful old buildings reflected the early glint of the sun, and the smell of fresh
coffee was in the air. Suddenly, the peace was shattered by a
strange and terrifying sound. Starting with a squeaking and a
rustling, it built up to a crescendo of screeching, and a frenzy of

furry, panic-stricken movement. The people of Kotor looked out of their windows.

'What is it?'

'I've never heard anything like it before.'

'Where's it coming from?'

'Look!'

'I do not believe it . . . !'

'Look, there . . . and there!'

The horrified townspeople saw a wave of animals scurrying frantically down the main street. Mice and cats and dogs, oblivious of each other and apparently intent on only one thing – getting out of town!

'What can it mean?'

'It's horrible!'

'Perhaps . . .'

'Perhaps what?'

'Perhaps it's a warning and we ought to leave too.'

The people didn't take long to make up their minds. Such a unique and frightening sight as they had seen seemed too serious to ignore. Within minutes the inhabitants of Kotor had followed the animals.

And at 7.30 am the first rumbling began – the rumbling of an earthquake. Within minutes its ferocity was such that the buildings were reduced to rubble. Clouds of dust rose in the air and fires began but, thanks to the warning of the animals, no one was hurt.

This story is a true story, and I have adapted it from one I found in *Assembly News* by Redvers Brandling (Hodder & Stoughton, 1989). It is called 'Strange Warning'.

Now, what would you have done, given such a strange warning? If you had seen and heard the animals, what would you have done? And what would you have done if you had heard John the Baptist, if you were living in his time?

John's Gospel does not tell us, but Mark's and Luke's do, that John the Baptist came as a furry sight, with a frightening sound. Dressed in camel's hair and leather, he yelled his warnings. He was a strange, wild fellow. 'Repent! Turn from your sinful ways! God is coming to set up His Kingdom. The axe is ready at the root of the trees! Every fruitless tree will be cut down and burnt! Flee from God's coming judgment!' He left no puzzles. His guidance was quite clear. It's time to change your ways. Stop cheating. Help the poor. Be content. Turn from evil. Turn to God. Confess your sinfulness. Be baptised. Receive forgiveness.

The common people read John's warnings clearly. Like the people of Kotor, they fled. They came from the rural area of Judea. They came from Jerusalem. Down the steep and winding inclines to the Jordan valley they came and were baptised, confessing their sins and receiving an assurance of forgiveness.

No doubt the religious authorities doubted John's judgement of some of them. Who was he to give a baptism of repentance? After all, he did not even claim to be the Messiah or Elijah or the promised prophet like Moses. Yet despite the leaders' doubts, the common people felt the impact. They knew that their repentance was genuine and they felt the acceptance of God. Perhaps they were like 36-year-old Svetlana. Her name was never entered in a register of baptisms, but she was baptised by an old Russian priest. Why? Because she had told him: 'God did not say that Christ cannot love me. He knew that Christ can love me, because he is the Christ. He heard my voice calling him and he answered me.' Who was she? She was Svetlana Alliluyeva, the daughter of Joseph Stalin, the dreaded and cruel Communist Party general. Yet, she knew when God had accepted her.

The events in the Jordan valley and throughout Judea were like a great revival, led by John the Baptist. Perhaps it did not go unnoticed that he worked in the same regions where Elijah and Elisha had led their great awakenings. The people sensed that something very significant was happening. Their lives were being challenged and changed. This man, John the Baptist, stood out.

That's my first point. John stood out clearly. It seemed at the time as if someone new came along every few years with a new idea or a new claim. There had been Theudas, who was not the Messiah, and people knew it. There had been Judas of Gamla, a rebel against the Romans. He had been executed. Now there was John. He was not anti-Roman. John was more anti-corruption. I mean, you do not call people a brood of vipers without thinking of them as dangerous, wily creatures, do you? It is as if he saw some of the Pharisees and Sadducees like creatures fleeing the effects of the scrub fires which could be seen on the banks of the Jordan when there had been logging. They were dangerous creatures, against which one should be on guard.

John charged some of these religious officials with insincerity. You can feel the anger in his soul and the creeps down his spine as he saw these 'pretend' repentants coming for baptism. His baptism for forgiveness, for them, would be no more effective than their circumcision in the tradition of Abraham had obviously been. The coming of the Lord would show up their true colours. After all, there was one standing among them, one who was to follow on from him, who was the true Light. In his Light everyone's true colours would be seen. And they still are. God knows whether we are a Svetlana or a Pharisee. John stood out in his day as the one to take note of. We must let our light shine, so that people may see the way we live and turn to our glorious God.

The second thing to notice about John is that he stood firm. In our short passage in John's Gospel, the priests and Levites who came to him were rather rude. In those days you did not just bowl up to someone and ask them who they are. You wouldn't bowl up to someone nowadays, would you? You wouldn't just say: 'Who do you think you are?' would you? But even if John could have taken offence at their approach, he didn't seem to do that. He simply took the opportunity to point them away from himself. He had been sent to give evidence about God's Light so that people might believe in Jesus. So he did. He pointed out who Jesus was. Would that we could make such positive use of negative experiences.

They wanted to stick some kind of important label on John, though, but he wouldn't have it. He stood firm. He was not Elijah, at least not in the way they imagined. He was not the promised prophet. Definitely not. His father Zechariah had foretold that John would be 'the Voice', the voice of one calling in the desert, preparing a straight path for the Lord.

Last weekend I saw my nextdoor neighbour out in the cul-de-sac with a brush and dustpan. She was sweeping the road, cleaning it up. Why? Well, by the thoroughness she was using, you would have thought that the Queen was coming, but she was not. Anne was sweeping up the leftovers from some tree felling she had had done. She was doing it to make it presentable to us, her neighbours. That's what she told me.

That is a picture of John's work. He had no doubt been aware from knee-high to a grasshopper that he was to make the nation fit for the coming of God's promised Messiah. Now he knew with absolute certainty that the Messiah had come. He makes that clear when he says he saw the Spirit descend on Jesus. Yes, Jesus was the one.

Are you firm in your conviction that Jesus is the Son of God, the one who is greater than John the Baptist, the one who baptises with the Holy Spirit? If not, I urge you to search for that certainty, pray for that certainty, take no rest until you know and believe of a certainty that Jesus is the Lamb of God, who takes away your sins; that He is the Light of your life. Then you will be born of God.

It is as necessary and urgent as the people of Kotor following the warning that the animals gave. When the Baby of Bethlehem comes again, as surely He will, we must each and all be ready, for He will come in judgement.

That is a serious matter. Aristotle said: 'We may go wrong in many ways, but right in only one.' And in the matter of our eternal salvation, we must 'go right'. We must acknowledge the Son of God, whose coming to earth we celebrate in ten days' time.

Now, to move on to my last thought about John, which is that he stood back. When John had made Jesus known, he stood back. He knew that he was not worthy to be the slave of Jesus. The New Testament often talks of Christians as the servants or slaves of Christ Jesus. Have you ever realized what a privileged position that is? To be in royal service. That privilege comes only to a few when we think of human royalty. It was Jesus who used the phrase, but John had the assessment right. Here was someone greater than Solomon. The hymn calls him 'Great David's greater Son'. John did not feel worthy to be in the employ of such a great and Messianic King. None of us are worthy, but that is what Christian folk are called to be. It is a tremendous privilege, which demands wholehearted and lifelong loyalty.

As another old hymn, 'Who is on the Lord's side', written by Francis Ridley Havergal in the nineteenth century, puts it:

> In the service royal,
> Let us not grow cold,
> Let us be right loyal,
> Noble, true and bold.

But let us not forget the example of John. Jesus must increase, we must decrease. We must stand back to let others see the glory of Jesus. It reminds me of one of those old weather indicators, where you had one character who came out for bad weather, but who had to go in when the other came out for fine. They could not both be in the limelight at once. And if we would make Jesus known to others, we cannot be in the limelight. If you look at Verse 37, you see that when John pointed out Jesus to two of his disciples, they left John and followed Jesus. John stood back and let them go. Let us all pray for grace to serve equally unselfishly, incognito if necessary, the Christ who came to make God's love known to us.

Let me end with another story. In the stable of Bethlehem, someone imagined the animals thinking and discussing: there was a camel and a horse and an ox and a donkey. The camel thought that he would have the most significant role in the new King's life. He would be needed for the King to ride, if he was to reach all the people of the world to save them. The horse thought the warrior Messiah would make him as famous as Bucephalus who carried the mighty Alexander in his glorious rides to victory. The ox thought that he would be most important because a King would have many riches to carry on many wagons, like David or the Queen of Sheba.

But they were all wrong. The humble donkey, who had felt too insignificant to join in the discussion, was the one who, 30 years later, carried the Messiah in his triumph to Jerusalem, where he died to save us all. It was the humblest, faithful servant who forwarded the kingdom. So, remember John the Baptist. He stood out as a beacon to point others to God's Son. He stood firm in the conviction of his specific calling and his faith in Jesus Christ. He stood back to let others follow Jesus and go on with Him in a life he was never to share. John ended his life of service in a prison, beheaded at the whim of a scheming woman. But still he speaks to all the world and points us to the Christ we cannot afford to ignore.

Trinity Sunday

Sermon preached by Edmund Hill at St Edmund's College Chapel, Cambridge, on Trinity Sunday 1996.

Fr Edmund Hill, 74, is a member of the Dominican Order which has a worldwide reputation for academic excellence. In his retirement at the Dominican house in Cambridge, Fr Hill is currently translating the works of St Augustine for the Augustinian order in the USA. He has already translated all of Augustine's sermons, which number nearly 500 in 10 volumes, and in fact submitted one of these to the competition last year but it got nowhere. He had better luck with his own sermon this year. 'Entering the competition was I felt a good thing to do,' he says. 'The competition is a very good idea.' Fr Edmund, born in Spain to a non-religious family, had decided in his teens that Christianity was 'a load of codswallop'. But the alternative philosophy he adopted fell to pieces when he was 21 and he began searching for something else. He tried the Church of England, but eventually the Roman Catholic Church was what appealed most. He was in the army at the time, and was received by an army chaplain. As a youth, he was told the story of how a cousin had been 'saved' from becoming a monk by an uncle, who pushed him into the Malay civil service instead. Nevertheless, his call to the religious life, which 'just came, somehow', persisted. He was studying history at Magdalen College, Oxford, and one day simply went to the Blackfriars house in Oxford and rang the bell. The door opened, and out came his cousin, who had remained in contact with the community he had wished to join years before. Fr Edmund, who obtained a doctorate in sacred theology, was sent to South Africa in 1966. In 1972 he came back to England on sabbatical, and was refused a visa to return. 'I wrote articles in the Dominican's monthly magazine New Blackfriars *poking fun at the regime,' he says. 'I wouldn't have thought that their people in government would have read* New Blackfriars, *but they must have done because they wouldn't let me back in.' He went instead to Swaziland and then Lesotho, where he joined the seminary staff in Roma and remained for 20 years until his retirement in 1994. To prepare, he reads the text for the Mass and gives it a few days' thought. On special occasions, he will write out his sermon. His Sunday sermons last up to 15 minutes, but the regular weekday homilies he delivers are 3 to 4 minutes long. 'Preaching is an essential part of the ministry and I enjoy it,' he says. 'It is proclaiming the gospel and sharing it with all the faithful people who come to church, and I hope encouraging them to reflect more on the faith than perhaps most ordinary Christians do.' He has in the past preached from a soapbox in the Bullring in Birmingham and in Derby. 'I was always floored in Derby by an old lady who used to attend regularly. She used to say to me: "Father – they do call you Father, don't they – Father, what do you make of what Jesus said? He said call nobody Father." I think she had a point. I have not resolved it yet. I suppose it is a sign of the influence of the world upon the Church.'*

Texts: In the name of the Father, and of the Son, and of the
Holy Spirit, Amen.
Bible: Own rendering of the Greek New Testament text

That should really be a sufficient text for a sermon on the Blessed Trinity, because of course this is nothing else than the mystery of God, the Father, the Son and the Holy Spirit. I presume – though I myself am only a convert, and cannot be certain of this – but I presume that this was the first religious utterance you were ever taught, you that had the good, or bad, luck to be brought up as Catholics. Even before you learnt the Our Father and the Hail Mary, you had to learn to make the sign of the cross 'in the name of the Father and of the Son and of the Holy Spirit'. Your very first introduction to God was to God the Trinity, Father Son and Holy Spirit, three persons, one substance.

But of course at that stage nobody, I imagine, talked to you about persons and substance, or even about three and one, or even about Trinity. None of these words, whether arithmetical or metaphysical, are essential to faith in the mystery we are celebrating today, or even to our desire to enter more deeply into that faith and to attain at least some taste, some savour of the mystery. None of them occurs in the New Testament (except possibly the word 'one'), because, after all, the mystery of God, of the blessed Trinity, is not a problem either of some kind of celestial arithmetic, about 1=3 and 3=1, or of metaphysical linguistics, about what 'person' or 'substance' really mean. It's the mystery of God being Father and Son and Holy Spirit.

There is, however, an excellent text for taking us, so to speak, into the heart of the mystery; it is Galatians 4.4–6:

> When the fulness of time had come God sent out his Son, born of a woman, born under the law, in order to redeem those under the law, in order that we might receive sonship by adoption. And because you are sons, God sent out the Spirit of his Son into our hearts, crying 'Abba, Father'.

Or more precisely, this text is showing us the divine mystery of God coming to us, sending the Son into the world as one of us, sending the Holy Spirit into our hearts, so that we may be taken back into the divine mystery sharing in the sonship of the only begotten Son of the Father, sharing in the Spirit of the Father and the Son, so that we may cry with the Son, 'Abba, Father'.

Now we celebrated the sending of the Son, born of a woman, at Christmas and Epiphany, beginning indeed to do so in Advent. We celebrated his being born under the law, to redeem those under the law, in Lent and Holy Week, as we moved up to the climax of celebrating on Good Friday the death by which he redeemed us. That we might receive sonship by adoption, we celebrated that with Easter and Ascension, when we were taken up into and with the risen and glorified Christ as members of his body. And of course we celebrated the sending of the Holy Spirit only last week at Pentecost.

The final effect of these sendings is the revelation to us of God as Father, Son and Holy Spirit, in whose name we were baptised, in whose name we cross ourselves, in whose name we say grace (if and when we do say grace), in whom we live and move and are (Acts 17.28). And the revelation of the mystery is crucial to our salvation, because sharing in the mystery, in the gift of the Spirit, in the sonship of the Son, as children of the Father, is our final destiny, in which our eternal salvation, happiness and bliss will consist.

So Trinity Sunday is very properly the Sunday immediately following on Pentecost. The Anglican calendar still follows the medieval practice of reckoning all the rest of the Sundays of the year until Advent as so many Sundays after Trinity, thus recognizing Trinity Sunday as belonging to the great liturgical cycle which celebrates the history of God's New Testament revelation of himself. The old Dominican calendar, before the liturgical reforms (in this instance, 'deforms') of Vatican II homogenized us all, followed the same practice – except that we were even more medieval, and reckoned those Sundays as the 1st, 2nd, 15th, 16th and so on after the Octave of Trinity.

The mystery, you see, as Paul tells us in that Galatians text, was precisely revealed by the sendings, the missions, of the Son and the Holy Spirit; missions and sendings that continue: 'As the Father has sent me,' our Lord said, 'so I am sending you' (John 20.21); sending us all, as missionaries in one way or another to the world, to mankind, to make disciples of them, baptizing them in the name of the Father and of the Son and of the Holy Spirit, (Matthew 28.19), so that they too may receive sonship by adoption, and cry 'Abba, Father' in the gift of the Spirit. So the Son continues to be sent in the mission of the Church, and the Holy Spirit continues to be sent into the hearts of men and women, to make them responsive to the mission of the Church – and thus by being continually sent, they continue to reveal the mystery of God, Father, Son and Holy Spirit.

So, if you are looking for more words than these three names to help you get some sort of grasp of the mystery, forget 'person' and 'substance'; they explain nothing. They were introduced in the course of the inevitable theological controversies to which the revelation of the mystery gave rise. Having changed their meanings in ordinary use several times during the centuries since then, they now only serve to mystify, to render the mystery almost totally opaque. No, the two further words you need are – mission or sending, and procession or coming forth.

The sendings of the Son and the Holy Spirit in time into our world of time reveal to us their eternal, timeless processions or comings forth in the eternal, timeless stillness of the Godhead; reveal to us the procession of the Son from the Father in his being eternally begotten by the Father, and the procession of the Holy Spirit from the Father and the Son in his being eternally breathed forth by them. It is in virtue of these processions that Father, Son and Holy Spirit are really distinct from one another. Because he is being eternally born of the Father, the Son cannot be the Father, nor the Father be the Son; because he is being eternally breathed forth by them, the Holy Spirit cannot be either the Father or the Son.

But because in eternally begetting the Son the Father is, in other New Testament terminology, eternally uttering his Word, his Wisdom, his perfect and complete self-comprehension and comprehension of everything else in that comprehension of self, the Son is equal to the Father, equally God with the Father. Because of what I called the eternal stillness of God and what the tradition calls his simplicity, his absolute incomplexity and changelessness, the Son is one God with the Father. And likewise the Holy Spirit, being breathed forth as the perfect expression, the very breath or sigh of the love of the Father and the Son, their love, their joy and their peace in themselves, a love and joy and peace that embraces everything else in embracing themselves, for that reason the Holy Spirit too is equally God with Father and Son, and is also equally the one God with the Father and the Son.

Do you now understand the mystery of the Trinity? No, of course you don't. Neither do I, neither does the Pope or Cardinal Ratzinger or Hans Kung or anybody else in this world. Only God can understand, can comprehend God. As for us, as St Paul says, we see now in a glass, in a mirror, and a distorting mirror at that, like those you sometimes get in a funfair; he calls it 'in an enigma', in a riddle (1 Corinthians 13.12).

But we look forward to the time when we shall see face to face. For we have been invited, by God sending his Son and his Holy Spirit, by his stretching out, as it were, his two loving and understanding arms to us, we have been invited to enter into that eternal divine embrace of God's wisdom and God's love.

Yes, that is what we should be looking forward to and preparing for as disciples and members of Christ, as the body of the incarnate Son; to enter almost as full participants into God's own life, into that eternal round dance, so to say, of the three divine persons in the stillness of the divine substance; to being introduced into that, our eternal bliss, when Christ hands over the Kingdom, hands over you and me and the whole world he has won, hands over the Kingdom to the Father, that God may be all in all (1 Corinthians 15.28).

Our Father, Who Art in Heaven

Sermon preached by Neville Manning at St Leonard's Church, Denton, East Sussex, on Sunday 16 February 1997.

The Revd Neville Manning, 56, trained at the London College of Divinity and was ordained into the Church of England in 1969. Earlier, he had briefly spent some time teaching. He served curacies in the Rochester, Chichester and Guildford dioceses, spent 16 years in the London diocese and is now back in Chichester as rector of St Leonard's, Denton, with South Heighton and Tarring Neville. One of his churches is 900 years old, another is 700. He has about 70 in church on Sundays and preaches nearly every week, being helped out regularly by two lay Readers. He goes through the lectionary at the beginning of every month, works out when and where he will be preaching and begins to think about each sermon. He spends a lot of time in thought and is one of the few preachers who uses neither text nor notes in the pulpit. With proper preparation, he says, he does not need them. He spends a week working on each sermon, writes a rough outline, makes headlines from these and then commits them to memory. 'When I first thought of being ordained, one of the things I felt drawn to was preaching,' he says. 'Maybe I was fortunate in the sermons I heard in my earlier days. I see preaching as a pastoral activity. It is part of wanting to share things with people, to feed them and nurture them. It is an integral part of worship.' Like most preachers, he rarely gets feedback from the congregation, although occasionally someone will comment when a point has shot home. 'People who don't go to church or hear sermons have a rather funny view of them, as though they are always deadly dull and to be avoided. This is sad, but probably does say something about the quality of some preaching that has gone on over the years,' he says. Neville, who is interested in railways and whose study is lined with model locomotives, is also one of the few clergy in the country who does not drive a car. He has never sat a driving test and often travels by bus or bicycle. 'This leaves me free to contribute frequently to the local press on matters of public transport,' he says.

Texts: Our Father, who art in heaven, hallowed be thy name.

Bible: Revised Standard Version

William Temple, who was Archbishop of Canterbury very briefly during the last World War, said that 'the great reality of life is prayer and all that is worthwhile flows from that'. The great reality of life is prayer – and if you want a goal or aim for Lent then it might be to grow in your own life of prayer or, in other words, to grow in your own relationship with God. And I know that some of you who have signed up for the Churches Together in Newhaven Inter-Church Lent House Groups will be thinking about prayer there together as well, following the theme of 'Pathways into Prayer'.

We find that Jesus in the Gospels was above all a man of prayer and that his whole life was lived in a relationship with God. All that he did was soaked through with prayer. And Jesus was clearly concerned that those who followed him should also share in that life of prayer. Because he knew it would never be easy he gave them things that would help.

One of the gifts that we receive through those first disciples is the prayer we normally refer to as the 'Lord's Prayer'. During our sermons at our Sung Eucharist here in Denton in Lent we are going to be thinking about that prayer, The Prayer Christ Gave Us. You may know that in the Gospels there are recorded two versions of that prayer. There's the one in Luke, Chapter 11, which is the shorter version. There's also the longer version in Chapter 6 of St Matthew, in the collection of Jesus' teaching that we often refer to as 'The Sermon on the Mount'. It's that longer version of the Lord's Prayer, the one which we normally use, that we are going to be thinking of in the Sundays in Lent.

The trouble is that we're sometimes so familiar with it that the Lord's Prayer becomes a kind of asset which we undervalue. You may have come across the story of a school assembly that was taking place some years ago and in that School it was customary to say the Lord's Prayer every morning. It's said that one teacher was standing beside a little child. The teacher listened as the child said the Lord's Prayer and these are the words which the teacher heard: 'Our Father, which art in heaven, Harold is thy name.' Presumably that little child had been saying 'Harold is thy name' day after day after day. And it's so easy, isn't it, to be just like parrots? The words flow out all too easily. What we sometimes need to do with the Lord's Prayer is to take it maybe just a little bit at a time, to reflect on it and expand on it. That's what we're going to do on these Sunday mornings, to look at the prayer Christ gave us.

This morning we begin with the opening words of the Lord's Prayer:

Our Father, who art in heaven, hallowed be thy name.

What that prayer does at its very start is to point us to the nature of the God to whom we are praying. And, as we are reminded, the nature of God is a twofold thing, almost like a coin with two sides to it. On the one side there is a sense of God's intimate care for us and yet, on the other side, there is also a sense of God's otherness, God's holiness.

Just think about those words: 'Our Father'. I wonder whether we realize the sea change that came for many people in their awareness of God through the example and teaching of Jesus. If we look back to the Old Testament we find that here and there are references to God being like a Father. Not many of them. There's one in Psalm 103 which we sometimes use in the funeral service: 'As a father is tender towards his children, even so is the Lord tender to those that fear him.' But references like that in the Old Testament are the exception rather than the rule. And it's only when we come to the teaching of Jesus in the New Testament that the picture of God as a loving Father becomes the predominant one. It was, of course, in this way that Jesus offered his prayers to God and lived his life for God, in a relationship with his heavenly Father. It's there in St John when Jesus prays his high-priestly prayer, not long before his Passion: 'Father, the hour has come.' It's there in the Gospels, even at Gethsemane, as Jesus faces what lies ahead and says: 'Father, if it's possible, let this cup pass from me; nevertheless not my will but yours be done.' Jesus not only realized that God was a Father but also wanted his own followers to share in that same kind of relationship. And it's that relationship which is ours through our faith in Jesus.

I find that when I pray, to remember that I'm praying to One who is like a Father is something that brings prayer alive. Because, you see, when we are praying we are not just praying to something or somebody we hope exists somewhere out there; we are actually praying to One who has revealed Himself as a loving Father to each of us. How important it is to realize that every time we pray! So we pray to God as Father, a perfect Father. It's been suggested that every time we say 'Our Father, who art in heaven' it does not mean there's a particular place where God is; rather, it's a way of saying that God is the perfect Father, because heaven and perfection in the Bible are linked. You may remember Jesus said that we are to be perfect, even as our Father in heaven is perfect. To say that we pray to our Father in heaven, I think, is a way of saying we pray to a perfect Father, and his fatherhood is not blemished in the way earthly fatherhood sometimes is. He is the perfect Father, caring for us as his children.

And so we come with that wonderful sense of God's intimate care. But the other side of the coin is what we might refer to as the Holiness of God. In the prayer we say: 'Hallowed be thy name.' In the Bible a person's name isn't just a tag by which they are recognized. To know somebody's name in the Bible is to know their nature and their character. To know the name of God is to know the character of God and God's name is 'hallowed'. God's character is holy, it's other than ourselves. And it's so important that we remember the note of God's holiness as we come to approach Him.

Nowadays, I suppose, in the society we live in we have lost that sense of certain things or places or people being sacred or holy, and yet sometimes we get near to it. I wonder if you remember the Christmas season when we had our Crib there on the Altar in the Sanctuary. At that time I often find little children going up and, as they stand in front of it, they look at it with their eyes wide and with a wonderful sense of awe; something like that sense of holiness as we come to God. Or maybe you go for a walk on the Sussex Downs and perhaps you see a marvellous sunset and you're filled with that sense of awe and wonder. There's something of that when we say, 'Hallowed be thy name.'

I gather that Lord Runcie was in a certain amount of trouble when during an interview he expressed his opinion that 'happy-clappy services', so called, were driving people away from the Church of England! I'm not quite sure that I even follow the logic of what he said and, to be fair, I think you'll often find maybe these are the churches where people are being drawn in. Now I'm not particularly a 'happy-clappy' sort of person, though

I thank God there is often a real freedom that we have in worship. But what I do think is important is that alongside that there also needs to be a sense of awe and wonder, that when we worship God we remember that we come to a God who indeed is holy.

I wonder if you remember the story about Moses in the wilderness, that day when he saw a bush that was burning. We do not know what caused it, but for Moses at that moment there was an awesome sense of the greatness of God and it was as though God was saying to him: 'Put off your shoes from your feet, for the place where you are standing is holy ground.'

It is so important that in our worship, alongside the sense of informality and freedom, there is also that sense of awe and wonder in the presence of God, that note we struck in our first hymn today, Faber's famous nineteenth-century hymn:

> My God, how wonderful thou art,
> Thy majesty how bright.

And so you see every time we begin to pray the Lord's Prayer we are taken directly to think about the kind of God to whom we are praying, a loving Father with whom we can have an intimate relationship, and yet also the God who is holy, before whom we come in awe and wonder. That's the nature of the God to whom we pray!

Happy Christmas

Sermon preached by Placid Meylink at the Monastery of Christ the King, Cockfosters, North London, at Midnight Mass at Christmas, 1996.

Dom Placid Meylink, 71, who is fluent in six contemporary languages besides Latin and Greek, has been Prior of the Monastery of Christ the King, a flourishing Benedictine community in north London, for six years. Brought up a Roman Catholic in Holland, he went to a secular school and then to agricultural college. His plan was to work in forestry in Indonesia. His call came suddenly. 'One day I was cleaning the pigsty and all of a sudden, I thought: "I want to become a monk, I want to be a priest." I put my shovel down there and then, and went to the telephone.' He called his mother, expecting to be summonsed home immediately. She advized him to finish cleaning out the pigsty and come home to discuss it at the weekend. He finished his course, and then ran into the monk, Abbot Constantine, who had prepared him for his first communion, who took him to Italy, where he did his novitiate with the Monte Oliveto Benedictine order. He was then sent to Louvain in Belgium. He came to England and joined the Cockfosters community 40 years ago, and attributes its success to being an urban monastery, where monks live the religious life but work and live in the heart of a lively secular Catholic and non-Catholic community. The aim of the monastery is to work for unity. Its parish church, a friendly, intimate building, has 1,200 through its doors at various Sunday masses. Thousands of retreatants, including many non-Catholics, visit the monastery for spiritual guidance and relaxation. Of preaching, Dom Placid says: 'My basic principle is that I want to be a channel for God's message. I always pray that at least one person will benefit from it, and if they do, I am happy.' Although he does not read directly from a text, he writes his homilies on one sheet of A4 paper, using a word processor, and preaches for 4 to 5 minutes. 'Preaching proclaims the word of God,' he says. 'It is nice to communicate what

I firmly believe in. I love it, but I always prepare, I never extempo-
rize. We are fortunate to have a very good congregation. They listen
very, very attentively. After Sunday mass we have coffee, and usually
people will continue to talk about the homily over their coffee.'
Dom Placid did not enter for the award. 'Our parish secretary told
me she had taped the sermon and she decided to send it in,' he says.
'I did not like the idea at all. When I saw there was an award for
preaching, I thought "This is silly." I still think it is silly, because all
preaching is God's word. But there you are.'

Texts: Happy Christmas
Bible: Jerusalem

You can well imagine how many lovely Christmas cards we
have received and we thank you. It was a joy to look at them
because they were all different: hundreds of them and each one
told me something about you. It was your message of friendship
and love, of hope for the future and of faith in this mystery of
Christmas.

I will pick out two cards for you to think about.

I particularly loved the beautiful nativity painting by the the
two brothers Antoine-Louis and Mathieu Le Nain from the sev-
enteenth century: the original you can see at Christie's and a
reproduction you can see on the cover of this week's Tablet:
mother and child looking at each other with locked gaze, the
mother tender and attentive, the baby motionless aud vulnera-
ble, with eyes only for his mother's face. With so many lovely
babies in our parish it was particularly beautiful to observe the
silent conversation between mother and baby, in this case of
Mary and Jesus: Mary wondering what this child is going to be
in the future after this very mysterious beginning and the utter
trust and love of the baby for his mother. We sing: 'Today, a
child is born and his name is Emmanuel: God with us.' Or as St
Paul comments in his letter to the Christian people of Colossae:
'In his body lies the fullness of divinity.' Here is a human baby;
here is a child with human nature and yet with a divine nature at
the same time. His name shall be: Emmanuel which means God
is with us.

But St Paul adds another tiny little phrase: 'In his body lies the
fullness of divinity and in him you too find your own fulfil-

ment.' That made me pick up a second Christmas card. It is a beautiful photo of a lovely girl whom I love very much. Her name is Paula. As you know she is a star in the theatre workshop Chicken Shed, in our parish. She is totally paralyzed, cannot walk and cannot talk. She is totally dependent on others and she sent a message to me, that she was able to write with the help of a computer which her mother then printed on a card and passed on to me. Paula, with her poetic creative mind locked in a paralysed, immovable body, writes with joy her Christmas message: 'Every day is special with wonderful moments. Christmas is one hundred of those days put in a box and given to you. Words of love Paula.' In Chicken Shed, Paula is able to be fully human and she is surrounded by hundreds of good friends. It is a privilege to have them with us just down the road. They are an inspiration and Paula is a shining star.

If Paula were here, I would say to her: 'Today a child has been born for you, Paula, and he is the Jesus who was alive among us for 33 years, suffered, died and is now risen. He is present among us now as the risen Christ. St Paul says that "in him you find your own fulfilment", even if that means that you, Paula, cannot talk or cannot move and must often be terribly frustrated. But you are alive and you are creative in your own small way; your life is a joyful hymn to God.'

I then ask myself what is this little baby offering to his mother, to Mary and to Paula and to you and me? He is offering freedom. That is what the people in the time of Jesus were waiting for – freedom and peace. That is what we are still waiting for: freedom for ourselves; freedom in Northern Ireland; freedom in Jesus' own country, Israel; freedom in South America, in Peru, in South Africa and many countries in Africa, in Bosnia.

Everyone wants to be free. But freedom does not mean that you can do whatever you like. There exists a false interpretation of freedom. Freedom goes hand in hand with responsibilities. A married person is not totally free where his wife and children are concerned. A friend is not totally free where his friend is concerned. A Christian is not totally free with regard to the Church as a community. A monk is not totally free in regard to his monastic community. No individual is totally free. You cannot be totally free from God.

If freedom is to be authentic, that is, genuinely liberating, it must make room for others, for fidelity to other people and even more to God. Our freedom is the effect of Jesus' obedience as a man. That is the mysterious gift at Christmas. That little child Jesus was totally free and yet when he grew up he repeated all the time that he came to do the will of God. He was obedient to his Father's will even to death. That is the challenge for you and me. The incarnation liberates us, makes us free but it does not work by magic. We have to fight for it.

We are continuously presented with artificial means of oblivion as a way of escaping moral struggle and moral obligation. A lot of pressure is put on parents and young people which curbs our freedom. Watch how most people celebrate Christmas. If you have the courage to enter on the path to freedom offered to you by Christ today, you will become certain that freedom and liberation are only to be won through suffering and humiliation.

That takes an act of faith. That was the message that that baby gave to his mother: you are totally free but you must think all the time of God's plan, God's will, as you did when the Angel Gabriel came to you and you said YES immediately. You have to suffer, you have to give your life even to death, but it will end with the resurrection.

Let us thank God for this mysterious Christmas present of freedom on this Christmas Day.

A Crucial Question

Sermon preached by Michael Parker at St Leonard's Church, Bedford, on Sunday 16 March 1997.

The Revd Michael Parker, 40, is rector at St John's, an 800-year-old Norman church in Bedford, and St Leonard's, a modern, multi-purpose church centre. More than 230 turn up for worship in the parish at three services each Sunday. Michael, whose wife Jane is a biology teacher, took a degree in chemistry, then worked half-time for British Rail and did a part-time lay training course at All Souls, Langham Place. He was ordained at 27 and spent 3 years in Norwich. He then went to Muswell Hill in north London and has been in Bedford for 7 years. He preaches once or twice a week, and prepares two separate sermons if he has to preach twice on Sundays. 'Sometimes it is easy to prepare, and sometimes I do it with great difficulty,' he says. 'I begin to develop some ideas about a month in advance. I put it down on paper at the end of the week.' He tends to follow a theme, although observes festivals and sometimes uses the Anglican lectionary. He preaches for 20 minutes, from notes. 'I particularly like relating to the text of the Bible and trying to make it relevant to people's lives today, to give it a cutting edge.' He is ambivalent about the sweat and sheer effort involved in getting to grips with the more difficult passages. 'Sometimes it can be just quite hard to find a good application that makes sense of where people are,' he says. He entered the award because he believes it encourages the art of 'good preaching'. He says: 'I like people to use the Bible well and rediscover its truth for living today.'

Texts: Mark 10.17–31

A rich young man asks Jesus what he must do to inherit eternal life, and Jesus tells him to sell all his goods and give everything to the poor.

Bible: New International Version

It is hard to know just what was going through the man's mind. Maybe as he had made his money he had learnt that connections were everything and here was another chance to have a few words with a person becoming rapidly famous. Maybe, like a lot of people, good though he was at his job, he was really quite shy and he had never quite had the chance to raise what was really on his mind Maybe it was that he felt a bit embarrassed about the question he wanted to ask. You see it was a religious question and for men, well, people like him, it was not the kind of thing they did. Maybe he was supposed to know the answer. Maybe it was meant to be unclear. Whichever it was he had hung back and let others make the running.

Now suddenly, in Verse 17, the man catches Jesus just in time. The crowd had thinned, Jesus was just about ready to go. The man asks Jesus a crucial question. In fact Jesus was going, about to leave and then the opportunity would be gone. But he just had a chance and this respectable, young, wealthy man pushed forward and asked: 'Good teacher, what must I do to inherit eternal life?' There, he'd done it and what a question! You could hardly ask a more crucial one.

This man had come to the conclusion that this world is not all. We live in a wider framework of eternity. It can seem unreal to hold such a belief in the latter stages of the twentieth century. Unless we can experience it, explore it, test it now, rationally and scientifically, then it cannot be, people often say. Notions such as heaven or hell are dismissed fast.

However, people deep down behave quite differently. When a new baby is born people sense something very special has happened. Just this last week one of our churchwardens has become a grandparent. Needless to say the new grandparents are excited; this afternoon they are off to see their new grandchild. No one would dare say to them, or to the parents, 'Oh don't make too much of it. All it is is another chance life in a chance universe, the baby has come from nowhere and its heading nowhere, it has no real significance. Don't make a fuss, it's only chance.' Those who passed such comment would be rapidly pushed outside!

Human life has that significance because this world is not all. There is the wider framework of eternity and the possibility of God to be known and experienced.

I wonder if you have asked the question yet, and have you got an answer that you are sure enough of, to rest your future for eternity on? 'Good teacher, what must I do to inherit eternal life?' It was a good question then and it's a good question now. Imagine how Billy Graham would answer, you can see that he would think the question a gift, or the Archbishop of Canterbury, or the Pope. They long to talk about eternal life. You might imagine Jesus would too. But look at Verse 18, see Jesus' astonishing reply: 'Why do you call me good, no one is good but God alone.'

The answer to the main question will be straightforward to understand, but a real challenge to put into practice. So it is important to know who is giving the answer, how dependable the answer. Jesus' identity is crucial. 'No one is good but God alone', he says. Jesus was good, very good. He would never be caught like some failed American TV evangelist; no tabloid investigation into him, no matter how powerful the telephoto lenses, would expose wrong. No matter how hard anyone tried, and some of the most powerful people in the country were trying extremely hard to bring him down, none would ever find any dirt to stick to him. He was good, very good, unlike any other person who has ever lived, perfect, and who is as good as that, God alone, says Jesus.

Let Jesus' goodness be one of the strands of evidence that persuades you to believe his claim to be the Son of God. Such goodness surely means he was not deluded and mad, nor out to deceive and bad, but was what he claimed to be, the Son of God, in truth. Perhaps you wonder if there is eternal life, life in heaven, life and relationship with God now. Jesus, in Donald Soper's words, 'the human photograph of God', says there is. Believe him.

So, before the main question there is this prior question. It needs answering if we are to trust his answer to the main question. The first question is the identity of Jesus, the second, 'what must I do to inherit eternal life?' But is eternal life in your sights? Sometimes I catch the round-up of the television viewing figures. *Neighbours, Home and Away, EastEnders, Coronation Street* are always near the top of the list, watched by 15 to 20 million people. Near them in the lists are the holiday programmes. They paint a picture of people massively absorbed by other people's lives. Is it because their own lives are rather limited, or people longing to escape their own lives to some warm, exotic place. Eternal life, life lived out in God the Father's presence, beginning now, fully developed in heaven, will bring colour to life now and the greatest future we can imagine.

It was a good question then, it is a good question now: 'Good teacher, what must I do to inherit eternal life?' But there is then a crucial change of priorities. The man has this question and he wants the answer. His sudden decision to break cover and come out of his shell and ask it of Jesus gives his question a certain edge. 'What must I do to inherit eternal life?' Clearly he is good. He claims to have kept the commandments for many years. Jesus does not disagree. But there is 'one thing more'. Jesus raises a delicate matter – money, wealth. He perceives where the man's security lies. It is not trust in God but reliance on wealth. Jesus sees his stumbling block for discovering eternal life, just as he can see ours. The man's face falls. Faith makes an impression on your wallet, your purse, chequebook, savings account, bank balance.

So then Jesus looked around and said to his disciples: 'How hard it is for the rich to enter the kingdom of God!' The disciples were amazed at his words. But Jesus said again: 'Children how hard it is to enter the kingdom of God! It is easier for a camel to go through the eye of a needle than for a rich man to enter the kingdom of God.' The disciples begin to think Jesus is crazy: 'Who then can be saved?' they say. We might add, 'Is the kingdom of God only for the poor then?'

'No,' Jesus responds, it is hard, but it is not impossible. 'With God all things are possible.' They really are possible and as a Church we see that. At least most of the time you could but do not because people keep their financial giving quiet and secret. The treasurer is aware of it, and those who reflect on where the money comes from to pay church, mission society, charity bills in this country and overseas. The reality is that rich people can become extraordinarily generous as they turn to Jesus Christ and take hold of eternal life.

I once sat on the council of a national body that had a member of the Royal Family as its patron. Someone suggested that funds could be raised from rich people who would be impressed by the person of the patron. It sounded somewhat unreal to me. However, I put the idea past a director of a merchant bank. He assured me that one of the main reasons the people suggested were rich was because they were good at hanging onto their wealth and they were unlikely to start writing big cheques all of a sudden to this particular organization. The director of the merchant bank is himself a Christian and an excellent example of someone who gives away a great deal of his money and is marked by his generosity.

'With God all things are possible.' We cannot measure our wealth or poverty just by comparison with others in this country. Our horizons have been enlarged by news programmes, missionary magazines and our own travelling. By world standards almost all of us have to rank ourselves among the world's rich. The underlying question in Jesus' reply is for us all. At root it is a question about security, about dependence. What matters to you most, heaven or earth? Which counts more, your standing before God or others?

Jesus perceived where this man's security was, so he said, 'To inherit eternal life, sell what you have and follow me.' In other words, Jesus must have the priority in our day, in our diary, in our chequebook, in our friendships, in our relationships. In some areas of life we will say fine, that is what I do and long for, just as the man in the account had kept the commandments.

However, for each of us there will be an area where our hearts sink, as his face fell; an area or issue where we say, 'Not there too Lord, how can I let you reign in that part of my life.' Coupled with the agonizing we will also say, 'I am not sure I can, it is asking too much, more than I can handle.' Then we need to hear Jesus' words to his disciples, 'With man this is impossible, but not with God, all things are possible with God.'

Before we conclude, see quickly in passing how Jesus' love for this man does not mean he avoids putting the tough challenge to him. Actually it is the love that leads him to put the tough challenge to him. Love does not avoid tough choices. Keeping the Ten Commandments falls short of giving any assurance that all will be well for eternity. It is a relationship with himself that Jesus offers. 'Come follow me,' he says. In other words, come live with me, be with me. Then assurance about eternal life will follow.

It is not just obedience to a set of precepts that Jesus offers as his gospel, but life, life for eternity. For the disciples, Jesus' call to the man has raised the whole question of material wealth and the life of faith. In the Old Testament two main views prevailed.

First, wealth was a sign of God's blessing; Abraham or Israel prospered as they did God's will. Second, was the understanding that the poor were pious and the rich were ungodly, more often expressed in the Psalms. Jesus' attitude is startlingly fresh.

Jesus goes on to promise that, however great the sacrifice, God will always make it up. They are verses that we must take care to understand. Jesus knew what he was doing when he made the promise, as did Mark when he compiled his material. It is not some slick prosperity gospel that someone who gives up one home will become the owner of three, or who turns his back on one mother will have a handful or mothers. We must not interpret Jesus so as to make him ridiculous. Rather, he says you will enjoy a wealth of new close relationships within the family of believers. You will feel at home in many places. Alongside all that will be the misunderstanding of others or, as he puts it Verse 30, 'persecutions'.

Peter, rash as ever, speaks out: 'We have left everything to follow you.' Jesus reminds him, be careful, many who began well, the first, will be last and will be overtaken by those who come to faith later. It is a warning to any established Christian to be careful where they stand in regard to their security and reliance.

Finally, there is the crucial question about how to inherit eternal life. Have your sights set that high and far. There is the crucial question about Jesus' identity. Let his goodness persuade you of his claim to be the Son of God and therefore to give an accurate, dependable answer to the question of being sure about eternal life. There is the crucial change of priorities. So come, follow Jesus, keep the commandments, set light to wealth, let the God of the impossible so work in you that you follow Jesus in every area of your life and let him enable you to bring the change where you know it is most costly and hardest for you. Jesus loves you just as he loved the man. He says: 'Come follow me.' Will you do that? Will you allow God to do what is possible for God but impossible for you?

Have the joy of knowing and following Jesus now and the assurance of eternal life ahead. There is no greater question than the one this man asked, no answer more important than the one Jesus gave. Let us be quiet and pray.

A Sermon Preached on
Advent Sunday

Sermon preached by Harry Potter to the King's School, Canterbury, at Canterbury Cathedral, on Advent Sunday, 3 December 1995.

Many modern clergy have given up high-powered jobs to follow their clerical calling but for the Revd Harry Potter, 42, it went the other way. He left the full-time ministry to train as a barrister and has recently qualified. Harry, a Glaswegian and a Presbyterian by birth, joined the Church of England when he went up to Cambridge University. He was ordained in 1981 into a curacy at St Paul's, Deptford in South-East London, but went back to Cambridge as chaplain and fellow at Selwyn College in 1984, where he taught Old Testament studies. At the same time, he began serving as a substitute chaplain at Wormwood Scrubs. After 3 years at Selwyn, he became a full-time prison chaplain and also studied for a part-time law degree, becoming one of the first graduates of Thames Valley University in 1992. He had to give up the chaplaincy to study full-time for his bar finals. 'I had a long-standing interest in criminal justice stretching back to my student days when I used to help with Borstal boys,' he says. 'I found I was more interested in prison work than university. Because I was middle class and educated, prisoners were always thrusting their legal papers at me. I often had the role of advocate on behalf of the prisoners. I enjoyed prison work a lot, but I was in danger of being promoted and would not have wanted that.' He now practises criminal law from Barnard's Inn Chambers, specialising in legal aid work, and is honorary curate at St Giles, Camberwell, where he preaches about once a month. His preparation is minimal. 'I wake up on the Sunday morning, have a cup of coffee and pace up and down. I found many years ago that if I did a great deal or very little preparation for a sermon, it made no material difference whatsoever in terms of the quality of the sermon. Sometimes I preach quite well and sometimes I do not, but it has nothing to do with the amount of preparation and all to do with whether the passage inspires me.' He believes preaching is important because it is one of the few opportunities people have to obtain help in understanding an aspect of scripture or theology. 'Most people are fundamentally ignorant about it,' he says. 'When you approach even a fairly educated audience, you never assume that a reference to the Good Samaritan will mean anything to them.' He is author of several books, including Hanging in Judgment, *a history of the relationship between capital punishment and religion in England, and is working on a book on piracy and another on the Earl of Moray, murdered in a feud in 1592. He draws some similarities between preaching and addressing a jury, the main one being the task of keeping the jury or congregation awake. 'I have been gifted with a loud voice and, because my mother is deaf, I have always had to shout at old ladies, so I am good at that.'*

Texts: Matthew 25.31–40
Bible: Authorised Version

In days of old, crowds larger even than this used to assemble at Tyburn to watch the condemned felon walk towards the scaffold led by an ecclesiastical dignitary. After he had mounted the steps a noose would be put round his neck, he would make his last speech to the impatient mob and then over a period of half an hour he would be slowly strangled to death. Well, I hope that this will not be my last sermon, and I can promise you that neither my death throes nor your agony will last for as long as half an hour.

'String 'em up!' 'Flogging is too good for them.' 'Lock them up and throw away the key!' You know the slogans spouted by the popular press and by unpopular politicians. They may well be sentiments you echo. In our society crime is the great fear, and punishment the panacea. Old Tories and New Labour vie with each other to be tough on crime and win the hearts, minds – and votes – of the *Sun*-reading public – all of us! Judges who used to be feared for the punishments they imposed and be immune from political interference are now criticized by press and politicians for being 'soft' on criminals. Prisons which were until recently condemned for their degrading conditions and for being the universities of crime are now held up as the only answer: more prisons, more prisoners, longer sentences, harsher conditions.

Today is Advent Sunday when the Church awaits the coming of Jesus in Bethlehem and contemplates the second coming of Jesus in judgement. So what does Christianity teach, what does the Bible say about judgement? The Bible is almost a textbook on crime and punishment. It begins with a crime and ends in a court. It begins with a crime: Adam is exiled from Eden and sentenced to hard labour for life, but God makes sure there are clothes on his back, food in his belly, and hope in his heart. Cain the first killer – and of his own brother – is branded for life, but the mark is for his protection as well as for his punishment. He lives to become the first city-builder, the founder of our urban civilization. It ends in a court, but no ordinary court, for the judge is prejudiced in favour of the defendants and even has a criminal conviction himself. The Judge is Jesus: Jesus who is also our advocate, our defence barrister, our brief; Jesus who was a friend of sinners. who told the parable of the lost sheep and the prodigal son, who taught 'Judge not that ye be not judged' and 'Turn the other cheek'; Jesus who was condemned as a criminal, crucified between two other criminals, and who on the cross promised a criminal that he would be the first Christian in paradise.

The Bible is Law but it is also Gospel. Divine judgement as revealed there has three characteristics. First, it holds out hope: no one is too lost to be found – not even Rosemary West and Myra Hindley. We can be born again. Adam is clothed; Cain is protected; the prodigal is reclaimed. Second, it looks to the heart: God sees not just the crime, not just the criminal, but the individual too: 'Man looks on the outward appearance but God looks on the heart.' Third, it is merciful. It gives as many last chances as it takes and then some: Jesus is asked 'How many times should I forgive my brother? Seven times?' He replies 'Not seven times but seven times seventy.' The Gospel this morning talks of Jesus judging not individuals but the nations. Our society, our nation, will be judged – as all nations are – by how it measures up to God's kingdom, by the quality of its compassion: and one criterion is how we deal with prisoners. Do we hold out hope? Do we look to the heart? Do we judge with mercy and give as many chances as it takes?

Take two contrasting examples. We are fast creating a group of long-term prisoners who have nothing to live for, other than vengeance or escape; escape out of prison or into drugs or through suicide. One such is the young man who escaped from Parkhurst last January. I have known Mark since he first arrived in Aylesbury at the age of 19. He was a university student and in many ways a brilliant all-rounder – artistic, musical, inventive. His background was complicated. He came from a middle-class family, but one with problems. Taller than most, odder than most, he stood out as an oddball at school and was the butt of many of his peers. He developed a grudge against and derision for humanity and used his brains to get revenge. He manufactured explosives, planted incendiaries, and badly burnt Leeds University chapel. No one was hurt during his whole campaign, but this was more by accident than design. Finally, on holiday, he fired two crossbow bolts into a neighbour's house when an all-night party annoyed him. The police were called and found not only the crossbow but an arsenal in his bedroom, and diaries outlining his actions over the previous few years.

On remand he began to change – he was only 19 after all – he became chapel orderly, began to get on with the sort of people he had never got on with before. Things began to sort themselves out. He expected 10 years – a long time for a 19 year old. He got 6 life sentences, a 14-year minimum tariff, and was made Category A, the maximum security categorization which severely restricted his movements even within a maximum security prison. Over the years despair has dislodged hope. All he lives for is to escape. It is, after all, the greatest virtue in wartime. They threw away the keys in Mark's case, so he manufactures his own. On his arrest he was dangerous, a risk to the public, but I do not believe he was a monster, nor beyond redemption. Perhaps now he is all of those things, but if he is, it is partly at least because we have made him so. If he is not, it is due to the triumph of the human spirit in adversity and the infinite love and power of God.

A very different tale is that of Jason, a drug addict and domestic burglar. He has been in and out of gaol all his life. He has to feed his habit and so he steals. Burglary – even by day – is considered a very serious crime, almost always meriting imprisonment. Last January he was given a last chance by the Crown Court. He would not go to prison but be placed on probation, providing he attended a residential drug rehabilitation project. Well, he did not. But this was not his fault. There was no place available. He still had a habit, he still had to fund it, he committed further burglaries. I represented him last month when he was pleading guilty to some seven offences – but how many had he committed? He should have gone to prison. No judge could justify not so sentencing him. But he did not. On the day he came up for sentencing a probation officer arrived in the court. He told the judge that that very day a place had arisen in the drug project, but it could not be kept open. His car was outside. If the judge were to risk it he would take Jason personally to the project and a month later he would return to hear his fate. With considerable reluctance the judge acceded to this request, but warned Jason that imprisonment in a month was almost inevitable. A month later he returned. His urine showed he had not touched drugs. He was making progress. The judge took a risk and give him another 'last' chance. It will almost certainly be in vain. Jason will return to his old haunts and environments, to his junky girlfriend, and get back on drugs. He will reoffend and spend much of the rest of his life going in and out of prison. That is what will probably happen, but it might not. It might not. This is just the sort of decision that the press pillories judges for. The judge was prepared to take a risk for what was right, and he was right to take that risk. It was the Christian thing to do.

As a society we have to judge and punish and imprison. But when we punish we must remember that we punish crime not sin; the thief not the selfish; the sex offender not the adulterer; the violent not the cruel. We must remember that we are all sinners and have fallen short of the glory of God. We must remember that we punish not ogres, not monsters, not statistics, but human beings like ourselves, and that there but for the grace of God and our families and our education do we go. We must remember that although crime is bad, inhumanity is worse. It is better to suffer crime than be a criminal; it is better to be murdered than to murder; it is better to take risks in doing what is right than play safe – or play politics – and perpetuate wrong.

When Jesus judges the nations and divides the sheep from the goats, he will do so not on the basis of the nation's gross domestic product, nor its per capita income, nor on the number of nuclear bombs, but on the basis of the quality of its compassion. Let us pray that on the day that that great division takes place and thank God it is not yet – that England (and Scotland) will find itself among the sheep, among the blessed, and that Jesus will say to us: 'When I was naked you clothed me; when I was hungry you fed me; when I was thirsty you gave me drink; when I was sick you visited me; when I was in prison you came unto me.'

'When, Lord, did we do this unto thee?'

'Inasmuch you did it unto one of the least of these my brethren you did it unto me.'

'And God Saw Everything that He had Made'

Sermon preached by Dilys Owen-Quick at St Mary's Church, Swansea, on Sunday 3 September 1995 and delivered again two weeks later, in Welsh, at Triniti Methodist Church, Pontard-dulais.

Dilys Owen-Quick, 81, was brought up in the Welsh Presbyterian Church but is now a member of St Mary's, Swansea, an Anglican church. She preaches regularly, in Welsh, to congregations of 30 people in local nonconformist churches, where there is a shortage of ministers. A retired geographer and anthropologist, for 28 years she was a principal lecturer at the Institute of Education in Swansea. She is also a regular contributor to local radio, providing regular Thought for the Day-style meditations. It takes her 10 to 15 hours to prepare a sermon, over several days. She preaches from a text, generally for around 15 minutes in non-conformist churches. Dilys has occasionally given the address in the Anglican church, where the congregation prefers shorter sermons of about 8 minutes. She has been preaching for 20 years. 'I regard it as a service,' she says. 'I never take any payment for preaching. I quite like it and I am used to public speaking, although I do not like to travel too far.' When preaching, she tries to address herself to the needs of the congregation. 'There may be someone there who needs particular encouragement or help,' she says. 'I try to throw new light on the Bible and create new interest. I really believe in what I have to say.'

Texts: Genesis 1.31

And God saw everything that he had made. And Behold it was very good.

Bible: Authorised Version

'And God Saw Everything that He had Made'

So reads the last verse of the first chapter of the book of Genesis. 'It was very good.' That was God's assessment of His work of Creation which concluded with the creation of Man on the sixth day, of Adam, made in his own image with a living soul. He represented the highpoint of all that God had made. God finally completed his work later with the creation of Eve, the wife and soulmate of Adam, for He saw that human beings need each other – that it was 'not good for man to be alone' – that we need society, that feature of human life throughout the world, through the ages.

Although God loved all that He had made, He loved Man with a special love. He accorded him special benefits. Food for his sustenance was ready to hand, 'all herbs bearing seed and all trees bearing fruit'. Adam had been given special status, a special role to play there in the garden of His bounty, 'to dress it, and keep it'. Man was given dominion over all living things, to care for them and respect them as the work of His hands. He was given freedom to enjoy all the good things that life had to offer, though within set limitations.

Adam and Eve were forbidden to partake of two trees in the centre of the garden, the Tree of Life and the Tree of the Knowledge of Good and Evil. As with all God's commandments, there was no deprivation for them in this. It was for their own good. In any case, He is with us in a real sense in His commandments. We have His companionship when we obey them. Society has discovered all too late in modern times that absolute freedom as an ideology creates anxieties. We are happiest when we conduct our lives within set parameters.

Adam and Eve thought otherwise, however. They disobeyed Him when they ate the fruit of the Tree of the Knowledge of Good and Evil. They rejected His right to arbitrate as to what they could or could not do. They created a discord between Heaven and Earth. They fractured their relationship with their loving Creator. Such conduct had, and still has as we observe in our behaviour today, dire consequences for human happiness on Earth. It had its consequences for God, too.

In the Genesis account it was Eve, of course, who first initiated that refusal to obey God. We may wonder why she did so, and indeed why we do so ourselves when we often wish it were not so. Yet, the forces that impelled her to behave as she did are all clearly revealed there in the third chapter of Genesis – a brilliant analysis of the springs of human conduct.

We observe the technique of the Beguiler. There was an initial 'softening up' process was there not? After Eve's all-too-brief recollection of God's law, he contradicted God's truth with the words: 'Ye shall not surely die.' He promised: 'Ye shall be as gods.' She began to wonder whether there might not be the possibility of status, power, glamour even, if she discounted the principle of obedience in such an apparently simple matter. Thus the seeds of disobeying God were sown in her heart. She looked at the fruit. It appealed to the senses, to feelings – 'it was attractive to the taste and good for food', 'it was pleasant to the eyes'. There was also apparently a good reason for taking it, for it made one wise and isn't wisdom desirable? Feelings and reason synchronized. 'She took of the fruit and did eat thereof.' She knew evil, and then became the tool of what was evil herself. The Beguiler was successful in his aim.

It is interesting to note how Antonio Damassio in his excellent book *The Human Mind*, also notes the importance of 'feelings' and 'reason' as factors determining the way in which we make our decisions to act. The dialogue which takes place between the two is of course instantaneous. Sometimes they synchronize, sometimes they conflict (as the Apostle Paul would confirm), and then the stronger force wins.

Adam, of course, broke God's commandment carelessly, with no verbal or mental reference to the Divine imperative. Characteristically like ourselves, he rejected all guilt on the grounds that he was intrinsically the victim of the 'situation in which he found himself – The woman whom thou gavest to be with me, she gave me of the tree', he complained. He sought to excuse his conduct on the grounds that another had been the root cause of his sin, in essence that his conformity to evil was due to the existence of evil itself. How much more involved could he get in his thinking in order to escape blame? Conformity of itself is not an essential guiding principle for conduct. Conformity to the moral law is what is required of us. Adam embraced evil when he chose not to do that. Also, we see that because both Adam and Eve were disobedient, though as a result of differing factors, that that first society in Eden became corrupt.

The Eden account is a most important part of Scripture for all of us. For too long we have treated it as an interesting story for children about an apple tree. It holds profound truths for us, truths that each generation needs to learn. It is a story for adults for all time, and perhaps one can say particularly for this age as it both warns and shows us how different evil forces and pressures can be used to beguile both individuals and society at large to act in a selected manner. Here many things spring to mind, such as dictatorships, eugenics, commercial advertising and even knowledge itself, as the world has learned to its cost in the case of atomic research, for example.

Jesus is our guide and pattern in this as in all else. He was subjected to the blandishments of Satan in the Wilderness, so soon after He had surrendered His life to God at His baptism in Jordan. Indeed what happened to Him there replicates the Temptations of Eden to a remarkable degree. He overcame all the Temptations of Satan by measuring them up against the background of His life's work for God. This was His instantaneous reaction as each attractive alternative was put to Him. Then the Tempter left Him abruptly. If we follow His path, unlike Adam and Eve we shall make the correct choice, whatever the matter under review.

Rejection of God's ruling had significant effects on the lives of both Adam and Eve as it has its effects on the lives of all of us if we choose to do likewise. They had surrendered the ruling grace of God in their lives. Their eyes were opened to a new world of evil. They had let it into their being. With the beginnings of death in body and spirit, and with shame and forebodings of sorrow in their hearts, they fled God's presence. They learned what it was like to be a sinner. Yet, if they fled from Him in their guilt, God remembered them. His eyes followed Adam as he tried in vain to hide himself from his Maker. God's voice reached him, 'Adam where art thou?' He called out as He still calls out to every one of us when we seek to separate ourselves from Him. 'Where Art Thou?' He called out. Adam's estrangement caused him grief.

That is the hallmark of Love. God still loved His human creation. Though they were to learn the consequences of sin, and He does not pull our chestnuts out of the fire, so to speak, He was there ready to help them solve the new problems that confronted them. Though no longer 'very good' there was still hope for them and life; eternal life was still to be within the grasp of mankind, through the Love of the Creator for him.

God intervened on our behalf and that intervention in His

great Love cost Him dear. He who is beyond all space and time, whose place is beyond this universe, humbled Himself and came to be with us in this world of space and time in the flesh in His beloved Son. In Jesus, the soles of God's feet touched this very Earth. He who was pure and without sin, not a prophet, but the Anointed Son of God – and we have no hesitation in declaring that fact, have we? – took Death, the fruit of our disobedience, unto Himself when He died on a Cross. He conquered Death, He conquered evil, and rose again. His sacrifice was acceptable to the God of all Righteousness as a propitiation for our sins.

Jesus freed us from the consequences of the presence of the evil within us and gave us eternal life instead of the Death of the soul, if we believe in His redeeming power. God loved His Son, yet out of love for us who had become flawed, He gave Him freely as a sacrifice so that we could be born again, recreated, reconstituted, our souls rescued from the sting of Death, kept from falling to be presented faultless before the Presence of His Glory with exceeding joy. Yes with joy, with the rejoicing Jesus indicated in His parables when the lost returned to the abode of Love and Care.

During this century in particular we have witnessed the increasing flight of many in our land away from God. Many that we meet are basically sad at heart as they ponder on the question as to whether life has any meaning. Most people believe in God, but they have little knowledge of Him and His great love for each individual soul. In our self-awareness we need a sense of the oversight of God in our lives. That is what keeps the human personality intact. It tears itself to pieces without it.

As Christ's disciples we must positively oppose the evils of our age and make known the great truths of our Faith among the young, the middle aged and the elderly. In this context we are reminded of the story of that aged tramp who said to Woodbine Willie long ago 'I would not like to offer God the fag-end of my life.' That remark betokened a sense of honour. But God would not have it so. We come to Him just as we are, at any age, at any time, to rest in the true happiness that He alone can give us.

Though we experience many joys in our life here on Earth, Jesus always reminded His listeners of the far greater joys of eternal life with God. It is significant that the closing verses of the New Testament take us back to the opening chapters of the Old Testament. St John gives us a wonderful picture of the New

Jerusalem when Evil has vanished for ever. There, nurtured by the waters of the River of Life which has its source in God and His Son, stands a new Tree of Life. Its leaves have the power to heal the bruises of sin, of the Fall, in each individual life, and all who come may partake of it freely and receive everlasting life. All this is ours through the amazing love of God for His creation, and the grace of His Son Jesus Christ, who gave His life as a ransom for the sin of us all.

What Could Eating Possibly have to Do with Your Faith?

Sermon preached by Machenry Schafer at McCracken Memorial Presbyterian Church, South Belfast, on Sunday 3 November 1996.

Machenry Schafer, 28, is a student at Princeton theological seminary in New Jersey, and submitted this sermon during a year's field study in Belfast, where he and his wife Katy, also a student at Princeton, were assisting Dr David Irwin, a well-known Belfast preacher, with his congregation of 800. Machenry, whose unusual Christian name is after his German grandfather, was brought up in the Church, but at university in North Carolina he became involved with a Christian organization called Young Life and 'made a decision' to commit his life to Christ. He decided to seek ordination while helping with youth work at a church in Florida. 'Northern Ireland is a tremendous place, it is beautiful and the people are beautiful,' he says. 'It is only a small percentage that cause trouble.' In Ireland, he preached about twice a month. Of all the preachers, his preparation was the most systematic. 'It takes an hour of preparation for every minute I preach,' he says. As most of his sermons last 12 minutes, he spends 12 hours preparing, over 3 days. 'I like preaching about something that God has spoken to me about,' he says. 'I like sharing things I have learned, or that God has taught me. A lot of my sermons have personal experience in them because I think that most people, rather than being theological, are common folk and identify with experience.' Like many of this year's shortlist, he dislikes preaching from a pulpit. 'I don't like being raised over the people I am addressing,' he says. 'I like being with the people. I like to convey my human side, and the way that affects my relationship with God.'

Texts: John 21.1–13

What could eating possibly have to do with your faith?

Bible: New Revised Version

This morning I would like to discuss a topic that is near and dear to our hearts, but probably even closer to our stomachs. The topic is meals: breakfast, lunch, dinner, snacks, tea, supper, midnight snacks, grub sessions, picnics, brunch, dining, a quick bite, a six-course extravaganza, or whatever you might call your meals. Meals are something that we all need and that we all have in common. We all spend a portion of our day wondering what and where we are going to eat, shopping and preparing the food we will eat, actually eating and finally cleaning up, resting and recovering from what we have eaten.

Many of my best memories are of my family meals. I remember cold winter days in east Tennessee, gathering with my family at my granddad's Methodist church in their fellowship hall for a giant feast with the whole congregation. I specifically remember going to the church's annual bean feed. Now I'm sure many of you are wondering what in the world a bean feed could possibly be? This was a huge southern event, where they would pack you into tiny seats with your family and give you a large plate with a mound of freshly baked corn bread. On top of the corn bread they would pour a motley conglomeration of every type of bean grown in the southern United States. Then you were expected to eat your fill and head back for a giant second helping.

The bean feed was never popular with a child like myself who lived and breathed hamburgers and chips. However, I always remember the fun I had talking and listening to my family that gathered for those bean feeds. We all have memories and personal family experiences around the meal table that are fun to look back to and remember. Katy, my wife, and I have already had several tremendous meal experiences and put on a couple of extra pounds while we've been here in Northern Ireland. But this morning I would like to suggest that the meal is a central part of our faith journey, past, present and future. If we look to the Bible we find that a tremendous amount of events takes place over the course of a meal. The Bible mentions meals or eating over 860 times. Certainly any religion that talks about food this much in their holy scriptures must be good.

But seriously, if we take a closer look at Jesus' life we find that a very central part of his ministry took place over a meal. For example, Jesus' last significant time with all his disciples takes place over a meal where he asks them to remember him in a meal-like ceremony we call communion. We also find several examples throughout the gospels of Jesus eating with sinners and tax collectors in their homes. Men like Zaccheus' and Levi's lives were changed over these meals. Jesus' miracles sometimes revolved around food, for example, when he changed water into wine at a wedding celebration and when he fed 5,000 with fish and bread. We also see Jesus incorporating meals into his parables and stories, for example, the Prodigal Son, where a feast is prepared for the son upon his return home.

These are just some examples of many areas of scripture that mention meals. Even after the death and resurrection of Christ, when the early believers began to meet, the original communion suppers were places where they could gather and break bread, share, laugh, cry and remember what Christ had done for then. This was all done in the form of a meal called an agape, or love feast.

So now we must ask, why were meals so central to Christ and the early believers, and why must they remain central to us today? If we look closely at a meal, I believe certain things are always present and happening. When we welcome someone into our home for a meal we are serving them and giving of ourselves. We are placing someone else's needs ahead of our own. Second, when we share a meal with others, we generally engage in conversation. We take the time to find out what is going on in another person's life and take an interest in who they are. In a sense, by taking this time over a meal to hear about someone else, we are saying: 'I care about who you are and what you're about.' Third, by sharing a meal with someone we are breaking the pinball cycle of life. Too much of our present-day life and schedule takes control of us and bounces us around uncontrollably. We do not have time to stop and slow down to find out how others are doing. A meal makes us slow down, stop and get off our personal rollercoaster ride long enough to reflect with others about what is happening in life. Sadly, in the United States, hectic lifestyles have almost destroyed the concept of a family meal. But by sharing a meal with someone else or having them over to your home, we are saying to that person: 'We accept who you are and we want to know you.'

As I look at this congregation, at the McCracken Memorial Presbyterian Church, in Belfast, I see that in many ways you believe that meals are central to the growth and warmth of a congregation. I see this at your monthly hospitality nights, at your light suppers following the evening service and at the way you always welcome people into your homes by offering a cup of hot coffee or tea. It is hospitality like this that I believe indirectly changes lives and welcomes people into the love and fellowship of Jesus Christ.

In the United States we have a programme in many churches across denominational lines called 'Logos'. This is where young children come together each week for games, Bible study, music and a meal. This programme was developed by the Church to help combat the eroding family mealtimes at home. Many adults and parents in the church come along to help lead and share a meal with the youth of the Church. One of the philosophies behind the Logos programme is having a meal together. This is stated as follows in their leadership manual: 'Meals are about . . . relationships, about righteousness, grace, justice, sharing, celebrating and providing nurture for one another. The dining doom is an arena in which leaders (and others) engage in risk, trust, commitment and vulnerability in relationships.'

I believe that the meal can be a place of reconciliation. When I was about 13 years old, I did not get along with my father very well for several reasons. We saw things very differently and we were gifted in different ways. He was excellent at finance and I was good at sports. His hobby was train watching and mine was collecting baseball cards and drawing. He was gifted at playing the piano and I loved playing basketball. About this time my Mom had decided to attend nursing school to pursue her second career. This meant that since Mom was not around for dinner and Dad did not know how to cook, he would walk with me to downtown Princeton, New Jersey, where I grew up, several nights a week to eat. As we began to share meals together and share our different lives, I began to learn new things about my Dad that I liked and even loved. A meal put my Dad and me on the same level. These shared meals between us brought true reconciliation and a better understanding of who we each were.

In Chapter 21 from the Gospel of John, I believe Jesus provided a meal for Peter and the other disciples in which reconciliation and restoration could take place. Surely there is a great need for it, for in the previous chapters Peter denied Jesus and the disciples deserted him in his hours of need. Jesus was taken by the authorities and the disciples did not see him again until he has risen from the grave. In the scene in John 21 on the beach, the disciples had gone back to what they knew – fishing. They probably did not know what else to do at that point. We see a familiar scene as the disciples fish all night and do not catch one fish. Then they are told in the morning by the unrecognizable Christ to throw their nets back in. Upon hauling in an abundance of fish, Peter is the first to realize that this man on the beach is Jesus and he jumps out of the boat in anxious desire to restore his relationship with his Lord. The Gospel of John gives us a beautiful image of Peter and the disciples being received by the risen Christ on the beach with a warm fire and a cooked breakfast. Of all the places Jesus could have chosen to restore his relationship with Peter and the disciples, it is over a hot meal on a quiet beach in the morning.

The meal can be a place of beautiful serving, accepting, giving, receiving, a place of reconciliation and restoration. As Christians, we are not just called to eat, we are called to eat together as families, husbands and wives, as a Church and as friends. We are people who have been designed by our creator for community. As you leave church, today I would challenge you to ask yourself two questions. Ask yourselves: 'How do I spend my mealtimes?' and 'Who could I reach out to in the name of Christ to invite to my dinner table?' Amen.

A Parable

Sermon delivered by Eric Sellgren at St Mary Iwerne Minster, Blandford, Dorset, on Christmas Day 1988, and later at St George's Church, Minneapolis, on 23 April 1995, after the Oklahoma City bombing.

The Revd Eric Sellgren, 64, is vicar of the Iwerne Valley churches in Blandford, Dorset. His group includes two medieval and two Victorian churches at Fontmell Magna, Sutton Waldron, Iwerne Minster and Shroton. His first career was in insurance, then merchant banking and shipping, but although he felt called to the priesthood by God in his teens, he did not respond until he was 25. His life was affected by attending an early Billy Graham mission. He was ordained in 1963 into a curacy at Wigan. He moved to Southport and then became warden of the Barnabas Fellowship, a conference centre near Blandford, before taking his current job in 1986. During his ministry, in 1971, he had an experience of the 'filling of the spirit' which made him aware that God loved him as a person. Although he is assisted by a non-stipendiary minister, 4 readers and 14 lay pastoral assistants, he still preaches at least twice and often three times each Sunday. 'This means I have to prepare three sermons. I use lots of illustrations, lots of stories, experiences from the past. Sometimes a sermon happens just like that, sometimes it takes ages. Sometimes I write them down, sometimes I preach off the cuff.' He spends two days in preparation for all three. 'Because I experienced the love of God as I did years ago, I want to try and communicate that. When it is done well, the sermon is a tremendous way of communicating the power, love and joy of Christ.'

Texts: Matthew 13.34

All this Jesus said to the crowds in parables; indeed he said nothing to them without a parable.

Bible: Revised Version

I've always been a terrible artist, and I suspect I always will be. The best I can manage is stick men, and my stick men are not a patch on L.S. Lowrie's. But one day, when I was 12, for my one and only time, I painted an excellent portrait. This is how it happened.

It was an art lesson at school and I was sitting at my desk trying to draw something that looked like a face, when Pop Fisher, the art master, came over and looked at what I'd produced. 'That's terrible, laddie,' he said. 'Look, do it this way,' and he proceeded to draw a face that was wonderful. Then he left me to copy his picture. Well, I tried, my goodness how I tried – but I couldn't. It just wouldn't come out for me the way it did for him.

Ten minutes later he came over again and looked and said: 'That's even worse! Now look, put your hand in mine. Keep hold of the pencil, but let me move your hand.' And then, together, we began to draw a portrait. At first it was difficult. I wanted to be in control, me drawing, not him. But soon he said: 'Look, lad, just relax and follow me.' And the strange thing is, the more relaxed I became, well, it was almost as if his power to draw began to pass through me. It was a strange and wonderful feeling.

In the end that picture was the finest picture I have ever drawn. I actually felt that if I could have stayed there, with my hand in his, I might have become an excellent artist. But I didn't, and I'm not.

In telling you this, I would like you to bear in mind that I have been strongly influenced by a remarkable similar experience which happened to the Revd John G. Williams, the broadcaster, related in his book *Thinking Aloud*.

My early experience later became a Parable – a Parable of what God wants to produce in my life, and yours, and the way He wants to do it. Let me explain.

Every one of us wants to be happy and fulfilled, to live a life full of meaning. The trouble is that, despite all our good intentions, something always goes wrong. It's always been like that, and I suspect it always will be.

Look at the world. It's a beautiful world. God made it so – but don't men make a mess of it: Northern Ireland, Israel, Bosnia, Rwanda, Afghanistan, the Sudan are just a few of the messes of the last few years. Ordinary people do not want war – they've had wars till they're sick of them – but no one seems capable of stopping them. Then there's the drug culture, paedophile rings, broken homes, broken marriages, child abuse, rape and murder. And isn't it sad that parents can't let their children wander freely today through the streets of our cities and out in the countryside as they did when I was a child? They're scared stiff at what might happen. Why should it be like this?

The fact is, as I have said before, we human beings have always been like this full of good intentions but incapable of living the kind of life we want to live, and incapable of changing. But God knows that this is so, and He has stepped into human history on three distinct occasions to set it right.

The first time He gave us the Ten Commandments. They were His way of telling us: 'If you want to live at peace within yourselves, and with each other, then this is the way to do it.' As the Bible puts it: 'Do this and you shall live.'

Well, we tried, my goodness how we tried. His chosen people, the Israelites, Jews, put everything they'd got into living by the rules, but they made two discoveries. First, they found that God's standards were far higher than they'd imagined and they couldn't live that way. Next, they found that they didn't want to live that way. They didn't have it in them. Oh, they did their best, they said – they did the bits that seemed right to them, but not the lot. We won't do what God says all the time.

When God responded by saying: 'You'll never be happy or fulfilled, unless you do', they shrugged their shoulders, gave up trying, and pushed Him and His rules into the background. And, do you see, that's where all these modern calls for a moral renewal in our nation break down. They give us the challenge, but they don't give us the power to do it – and we can't do it on our own.

Which brings us to the second and third times that God stepped into human history. The second time He came in Jesus. In Jesus, God came to live an ordinary human life, just like yours and mine, But this time it was not a case of giving us some rules to live by. It was not even a matter of showing us what to do. In Jesus, God was saying: 'This is how I want you to live, and soon I'll give you the power to live that way.'

And that's what happened on the Day of Pentecost. On that day, 2,000 years ago, 120 men and women, waiting in an Upper

Room, said 'yes' to God when He asked them to let Him do anything He wanted with their lives. On that day, the third time He had burst into human history, as they felt God's living power flow into them, it was just as if His Spirit entered them, the Spirit of Jesus, saying: 'Relax – stop striving to do it yourselves. Follow Me – put your hand in Mine.' And the more they did, the better the picture became. They reproduced the face of Jesus.

The Good News is that it's still happening today. Today, when we say 'yes' to Jesus, and place our hands in His, we become excellent artists, adding to the picture that God had in mind when He laid out His blueprint for the world. 'Abide in me and I in you,' he said. The more we do, the more His life pours in, and on and out into the world, so that the world is changed, and becomes more like God intended it to be – a masterpiece.

Faith and Fear

Sermon delivered by Lorna Sivyour at Angmering Baptist Church, West Sussex, on 15 October 1995.

Lorna Sivyour, 51, is a violin teacher who is also a lay preacher in her local Baptist church. The congregation of about 90 includes 3 other lay preachers and several retired ministers, so there are not as many opportunities to preach as she would like. Her husband, David, is a marketing manager. When they met, she had been widowed and he was a widower. They have 5 children between them, by their late spouses. Lorna grew up in Epsom, Surrey, in a non-churchgoing but Christian family. She was converted at 13 when she went to a Christian meeting in a marquee in Surbiton, and has been a Baptist ever since. She is currently Women's President of the Sussex Baptist Association and speaks regularly at Baptist meetings. 'I prepare through prayer and studying the Bible,' she says. 'My husband and I go out for long walks and that inspires me.' She was widowed in 1976, when her daughter was only three months old. 'So many elderly ladies are bereaved. I can help them by describing how God has helped me personally,' she says. 'I preach as the Holy Spirit moves me. I preach for about 20 minutes. I am just so grateful to God, that He has given me the opportunity to speak to people who do not know him. I do believe people can be touched or moved, by a a prayer, a hymn, by the Holy Spirit. But once you have been converted, you have to be fed on the Word. You must have a good preacher to feed you all the time.'

Texts: Hebrews 11.6
Bible: New International Version

How is our faith this morning? Are we pleasing God? Without faith it is impossible to please God. How are we coping with the enormous pressures, strains and stresses of living in 1995? I'm not talking about the little problems, the minor irritations of everyday. I think we would all say that we have some of those.

There was a young man who has just been converted to Christianity and he went to his minister and said: 'Oh, I've got so many problems. I thought when I became a Christian, I wouldn't have so many problems.' And the minister turned to him and said: 'I'll take you to see 15,000 people who haven't got any problems.' The young man thought: 'I'm going to get my answers now.' They put their coats on – the man was very intrigued – and off they went. And they went to the cemetery, they went to the graveyard.

The man believed that we all have problems every day, but I'm not talking about those this morning, I'm talking about the relentless, persistent problems which won't go away. It's as though, suddenly, a veil has come across the future. It's as though we're boxed in. We just cannot think of the future. Are these problems grieving us, are they making us discontent, are they making us resentful, bitter? Or are we growing in those times, growing to be more like Jesus? One member of our church talked about pain a few weeks ago and he said that pain of any sort has a place in our lives. So are we growing?

I was going to go through the seven ages of man, but I think the majority of us are over 30, so we'll start from that age. Between 30 and 40, your husband might be made redundant, so things do not look too good there. Or the wife might lose her job and health, how are we going to keep up the mortgage payments? The future looks really, really bleak, a veil has come across the future.

At 40 to 50 the children start to leave home, and where are the husband and wife? Ooh, who are you? Ooh, who are you? They don't know each other. They haven't built a relationship while the children were growing up, and, suddenly, they've got to build up a relationship again. What's going to happen in the future?

At 50 to 60 there might be elderly parents on the scene. It might be: 'I'm worried about my mum. She has not been very good these last few days, and I'm wondering what will happen? Will she go into a home? Could we have her with us? And your dad's not very good, I'm not sure what will happen there.' This veil has come across the future.

At 60 to 70 I'm really worried about my partner – a husband

or a wife who has not been really very good lately. Supposing she dies before me, or supposing he dies before me, what will happen, how will I cope? I know I'm a Christian, I know I am going to heaven, but I am still a bit frightened about dying. I'm not sure how I'm going to cope, I do not really want to suffer. How am I going to die? And a veil has come across the future.

We know, don't we, if we've lived long enough and we're Christians, and we look back and think, we have been in one of those sorts of situation before, and God has helped us. We've been there, we know in our minds, don't we? We also know about Jesus and God being the potter and us the clay. We know about the oyster and how the beautiful pearl is made, because the oyster decides to get rid of this sand that is in its shell and it starts to make this fluid and it has this irritation, and suddenly this beautiful pearl is made. We know that in our minds, don't we? But, it's not only knowing it in our minds, we must know it in our hearts. When you pray, and perhaps it might only be one or two of you in these situations, but when you go out of this door I pray that one person at least will go away released from his or her own fear. You know it in your hearts as well as in your minds.

It might be that we don't know about the future. If I'd known about this, and I don't want to go on about this for too long, but in my view, in 1977, if I'd known what those first six months were going to be like, I would have collapsed in a heap on the floor. Those first six months, seven months, seemed like a hundred years. My daughter, who was only about three months old, was in hospital. My husband was in hospital with a heart attack. He died in the March, and my mother-in-law died the following June; all that in a period of six to seven months.

But I did learn one important lesson. We have only have today. We have to learn to live one step at a time. We mustn't rush into the future. We have to learn to live in that present moment and then rest in the Lord. We mustn't let our circumstances, whether good or bad, dictate our view of God. If we think what is happening is God's way, then it won't be so long before we're fearful and anxious, thinking, oh, I'm a bit doubtful about God, perhaps he's somewhere else.

I've got a two-sided coin, one side is fear and one is faith. Fear is the dark room where negatives are developed. It is obviously the other side of faith, and fear in your mind can obviously start to affect your body, your hand is trembling, your heart moves faster, and your knees shake, and you turn white.

The mind has an effect on your body. Why is it, and I don't know what the statistics are, but why is it that so many people are on anti-depressants, so many people suffer panic attacks, agoraphobia, the fear of failure, the fear of disease, unemployment, fear of what others think about you. They all poison our inner peace.

In the *Baptist Times* in June, there was an article called 'Release From The Spirit of Fear'. It said: 'As we celebrate again in our churches the coming of the Holy Spirit, is it perhaps release from fear that we need more than anything else?' There are few more crippling or debilitating conditions than fear. Failure, fear of change, fear of the unknown, fear of losing faith, such fears can paralyze a whole church, just as they can a single individual. The coming of the Holy Spirit released the early followers of Christ from their fear and that must surely be our prayer for those of us who are his followers today.

So what is the anti-toxicant for fear? There are four. First of all there is prayer, absolutely loads and loads of prayer, just soak yourself in prayer. David prayed seven times a day, he didn't take tea breaks, coffee breaks, he took prayer breaks. Whenever that fear comes into mind, pray, turn your eyes on Jesus, away from that circumstance.

The second is loads and loads of Bible reading. Perhaps we ought to be taking our Bibles out on the trains and out into the country, and reading, and soaking our minds in verses. There are, apparently, and I've been reading about this, 350 'fear nots' in the Bible. Now, sadly, I didn't find 350, I could only find 60. But perhaps that is something you could do, try and find me 350 'fear nots'. One every day, or nearly every day. We spend a lot of money on our bodies, on vitamin pills – how about taking one of these every day, fear not. Perfect love, casts out fear.

And third, worship: go to church expectantly, go to church knowing that Jesus is going to talk to you, that God is going to speak to you. Listen to what he has to say to you. It might not be in a message, it might be in a prayer, in a hymn, or just as you are sitting there, listening to what Jesus is saying to you.

Last, hold on to the vision. As we heard here before in another sermon, we can help Christ with the constant love of the believer in Jesus. We must hold on to hope and never let it go. So that's the four: prayer, Bible reading, worship and vision.

Now I'd like us to do something slightly different. I'd like us to bring our fears before God. Nobody else knows what you're fearing at this moment, perhaps it might only be one or two of you. But just fire ahead, and bring that fear before God. Now I'm going to read some Bible verses. I'm going to say them, and I'd like you to repeat them afterwards. But first can we just bring that fear before God. We must obviously confess any sins. God is not going to listen if we are still sinning in our hearts.

> I am the Lord thy God. I have loved thee. Fear not for I am with thee even everyone who calls my name, for I have created them for my glory.

> But now is the Lord who created me. Fear not, for he has called me by my name. I am his. When I pass through the waters, the Lord will be with me. When I walk through the fire I will not be burned. I am precious in his sight and he loves me. Fear not, for the Lord is with me.

That fear has gone. Don't allow it to come in, don't let the devil attack you. When we walk out of the door we know that that fear has gone.

What is faith? The dictionary term is reliance, trusting, belief founded on authority, and what greater authority have we than God? Faith as the Bible defines it is a present tense action, evidences of things unseen, in God's promises, and acting on them today. It's the essence of which great people of faith are made. Faith is like a muscle, it grows with exercise, gaining strength over time. As I said before, we spend millions on the health of our bodies, jogging, exercising, dieting, but only the spirit is going to live on, and not the outer body.

A friend who worked as a missionary in inland China said this, and he's among great difficulties and pressures. 'It does not matter how great the pressure is, what really matters is where the pressure lies, whether it comes between you and God, or whether it presses you nearer to his heart.' We must be faithful regardless of circumstances. God always rescues those who are true to him. Indeed our relationship with God deepens only when we have worked through the disappointment, the confusion, and the bewilderment. God is chipping away to make a stone which will fit perfectly in the great temple of heaven.

As we heard in our readings from Hebrews 11, Abraham was a model of faith. For 175 years this great man lived, but there wasn't anything written about his first 75 years. And the remaining 100 years is only 12 chapters, a few blossoms of faith, courage, and consolation. Yes, he was the model of faith, but what was this spiritual giant doing through the rest of his life? Routine caring for his family, daily duties, and going for long periods without any spiritual mountain-top experiences. But he spent his time with God, in prayer, building up a relationship with God, and so it is with us. The eternal significance of our lives probably consists of a very few, short moments, separated by long periods of just ordinary existence. If the saints of the Bible were ordinary people of faith, then we, too, can do great things for God. God's people are ordinary folk, with duties, just like you and me but how they live and what they do has meaning for eternity.

Let's go back to that boxed-in feeling for a moment. There's a wonderful story for you in the Ten Commandments with Moses. There he is right in front of the Red Sea with Pharaoh chasing him, and he knows God is going to help him. But can you imagine? He's coming against this wall, this sea, with these people behind ready to kill him. Can you imagine the panic, the mayhem, the men saying where is God now, where is he now and the women screaming? They watched as God delivered a path through the sea and destroyed the greatest army on earth before their very eyes.

An amazing faith can turn that Red Sea into a beautiful red carpet. In the Psalms we read that the way is in the sea. God's character has not changed, his power has not changed. He will be with us. But when we notice in that story, in Exodus 14, when Moses was there, with this boxed-in feeling, it says: be still. Faith is not a last resort, it is a way of life, an entire reliance on Jesus. Faith is just to rest in him, to let him in, to rest in this love.

A Woman Accused of Adultery

Sermon preached by Julian Templeton at St Andrew's United Reformed Church, Iver, Buckinghamshire, on 11 August 1996.

The Revd Julian Templeton, 29, whose part-Maori wife Roimata is a professional opera singer, trained for the ministry with the Presbyterian Church in New Zealand, where they both come from. In New Zealand it is traditional for young adults to travel a year or more before settling down. Shortly after his training finished, Julian came to England with Roimata, who holds a British passport, which means they can stay here as long as they wish. Julian was brought up as a churchgoer and felt called to the ministry from his late teens. Like many New Zealand Christians, he has been strongly influenced by the charismatic revivalism which has swept parts of the world in the last two decades. 'I was prayed for, for the baptism of the Holy Spirit, and I felt an incredible warmth, and a sense that God was real,' he says. 'There followed from that a real wanting to praise and serve God. It was a very dramatic experience and it was not long after that that I felt this call to train for the ministry.' He is part-time at his Iver church, and preaches three times a month, combining his ministry with postgraduate studies in theology at King's College, London. After he has gained his doctorate, he might seek to become a lecturer. He is assisted by a grant from the United Reformed Church, which has a tradition of academic excellence which has dedicated funds to encourage more ministers to pursue theological study. To prepare, he studies the lectionary text for the week and reads commentaries and other works. He looks for contemporary stories and ideas to make the passage fit into contemporary context. He spends 10 or 12 hours over several days, finally typing it into a word processor. He hopes to be confident enough one day to work from notes. 'Preaching is an amazing privilege,' he says. 'The challenge is first to grab people's attention, and then to help them listen and think about what God wants them to do with their lives. Even if people do not agree with what I have said, if I have made them think I have achieved something. The sermon is perhaps one of the few times when people actually sit down for any length of time to listen to a reasoned presentation of something. God is often pushed to the margins these days. Preaching is vital in trying to bring God back from the margins and more into the centre of life.'

Texts: Exodus 34.4–9; John 8.1–11

Let he who is without sin be the first to cast a stone.

Bible: Revised English Bible

In our story from John a woman is brought before Jesus who is charged with committing adultery; yet Jesus refuses to pronounce her guilty. 'Neither do I condemn you; go and sin no more.' A dangerous precedent, surely? Letting a wrongdoer get off scot-free must contribute to the lowering of moral standards? In fact, the Early Church was not quite sure what to do with this story. In most translations it appears at the beginning of John Chapter 8, but in others it appears in brackets at the very end of the Gospel. The uncertainty about where to put the story reflects a wider uncertainty about its authenticity. In style and vocabulary it is completely unlike the rest of the Gospel and is actually omitted in the earliest and most reliable Greek manuscripts. Added to this, the earliest Greek commentary on the story we have dates from the 10th century AD. As it stands, the story reads as if it could have been written by Luke rather than John. It is almost certainly a later insertion into the Gospel by a different writer.

Having said that, even if it was not written by John, it shows all the signs of being an authentic story, based on an actual event in the ministry of Jesus. The compassionate attitude of Jesus to the woman is consistent with much of his other teaching such as: 'I have come to save sinners, not to condemn them.' 'Do not judge others, or you too will be judged.' and 'Take the plank out of your own eye before trying to take the speck out of your brother's eye.'

The first question that always arises for me when I read this story is this. We know who the adulteress in this story is, but who is the adulterer? The scribes and Pharisees bring a woman only before Jesus who has been caught committing adultery. But she certainly did not commit adultery by herself, so where was the guilty man? Had he escaped? Or was he let off the hook? Certainly according to the Torah the man was equally as guilty as the woman in matters of adultery. Leviticus 20.10 states that if a man commits adultery with the wife of his neighbour, both the adulterer and adulteress shall be put to death. In Deuteronomy 22, the penalty in the case of a girl who is betrothed to be married caught in adultery is that she and the man who seduced her are to be brought outside the city gates and stoned to death. But in our story we have the woman and not the man. So straight away the incident is weighted unjustly against the woman, for there is not mention at all of the adulterer.

Was the woman married or betrothed to be married? There are two possibilities. First, the woman was already married. The problem with the first possibility is that the penalty for adultery for a married woman was death, but the method of death was not specified. But the scribes and Pharisees in our story state that according to the law the woman should be stoned. In which case we may be looking at our second possibility; the woman may have been betrothed to be married. If this is the case then this story takes a much more sinister and unsavoury turn. The usual age of betrothal for a Jewish woman was 12 years of age. So it is possible that the scribes and Pharisees actually bring a 12-year-old girl before Jesus who has probably been seduced by an older man, and they put it to Jesus that because she has been caught in the act of adultery she should be stoned. However, whether she was married or betrothed to be married aside, what is clear is that somehow she has been caught committing adultery.

The reason the scribes and Pharisees bring the woman before Jesus is because they wish to test and trap him. They place Jesus in a dilemma. On the one hand, if he condemns the woman then they can say that he is not the friend of sinners after all and he would also be guilty of breaking Roman law; for in Roman-occupied Palestine only the Roman legal system could pass a death sentence. On the other hand, if Jesus pardons the woman, then the scribes and Pharisees could accuse him of encouraging others to break the law of Moses and also of condoning and even encouraging adultery. So clearly, the woman is brought before Jesus as a test.

'Teacher,' they say, 'the law of Moses says that such women are

to be stoned. What do you say about it?' But even in this asser-
tion they distort the law, which states that both the woman and
the man should be stoned. Jesus does not respond immediately
to their question, but stoops down and begins to write on the
dusty ground with his finger. Why did he do this? Was he simply
doodling, and playing for time? Was he bending over in an
attempt to suppress his anger at the actions of the Pharisees? Or
was he actually writing something of significance on the dusty
Palestinian ground? One suggestion is that the woman caught in
the act of adultery was not a chance discovery at all, but that the
whole thing had been set up beforehand. For a charge of adultery to be brought there had to be two witnesses, so the suggestion is that the witnesses had been planted and the whole thing
had been specifically connived to trap Jesus. Now, if Jesus was
aware of this, it could be that he was writing in Hebrew a quote
from Exodus 23: 'You shall not support a wicked man as a malicious witness.' Whatever he was writing, he does not respond to
their question immediately.

The scribes and Pharisees continue to question Jesus, so he
stands up and says: 'Let the man who is without sin be the first
to cast a stone.' And then he stoops over again and continues
writing on the ground. Silence. No one in the accusing crowd
says anything. But gradually, beginning with the older men, one
by one they begin to leave. What had Jesus said? What had he
done in one short sentence? Brilliantly, he had evaded their trap,
he had not condemned the woman, but neither had he pardoned
her, at least, not yet. For Jesus had cleverly turned their accusa-
tion back upon themselves: 'Let him who is without sin be the
first to cast a stone.' Jesus effectively said to the woman's
accusers, 'Yes, you may stone her – but only if you have never
ever contemplated adultery yourselves.' And straight away we are
reminded of Jesus' revolutionary teaching: 'Whoever looks at a
woman lustfully has already committed adultery with her in his
heart.' The members of this lynch mob thought they had a clear
case of a sinner caught in the act who must be condemned. But
Jesus turns the tables on them and forces them to examine the
purity of their own thoughts, motive and desires. And one by
one they acknowledge that they are all sinners to some degree.
The older and wiser ones realize this first and leave, followed by
the younger hotheads, until Jesus and the woman are left completely alone. There is no one without sin to cast the first stone.

Then Jesus says to her, 'Where are they? Has no one condemned you?' The woman answers, 'No one, sir.' Jesus replies. 'Neither do I condemn you; go and sin no more.' What had Jesus done here? He had offered this woman the possibility of redemption, the possibility of a new start. He refused to condemn her, but neither did he condone what she had done. He called adultery what it was, sin, and told the woman not to do it again. But in doing so he was inviting her to adopt a different lifestyle for the future by not repeating the mistakes of the past.

The scribes and Pharisees did not treat the woman as a person; she was merely a pawn in their game in which they hoped to checkmate Jesus. But Jesus refused to allow the woman to be exploited or dehumanized for the sake of a legal test. Contained in his words 'Neither do I condemn you' was forgiveness. Contained in them was grace. And grace, by definition, is always undeserved. So what we have in this story is the contest between law and grace. In the law as the scribes and Pharisees understood it, the woman should have been condemned and stoned. But Jesus believed in grace, and therefore thought the woman should have a second chance. What Jesus realized, but what the scribes and Pharisees could not see, was that the very basis of the law is grace. According to our reading from Exodus, when Moses stood on Mount Sinai with the stone tablets upon which the Ten Commandments were written, the Lord appeared to Moses and told him that He was God who was compassionate and gracious, long-suffering, ever faithful and true, remaining faithful to thousands, forgiving rebellion and sin but without acquitting the guilty.

Compassionate, gracious, forgiving; this is the God who Jesus knew and taught about, but this was a world away from the legalistic God of the scribes and Pharisees. Contained in Jesus' refusal to condemn the woman was grace and forgiveness. But equally contained in his words 'Go and sin no more' was also a challenge. Jesus confronted this woman with the challenge to change. He did not say 'It's alright, don't worry, carry on as you are', for Jesus recognized how destructive infidelity could be in marriage. No, he told the woman to stop what she was doing, and challenged her to change her ways. Go and sin no more.

This story touches on a number of present-day hot potatoes: sexual morality, marital faithfulness, the treatment and rehabilitation of offenders. This story warns us against being too quick to take the moral high ground on matters of sexual morality. We may have strong views on such issues as sex outside of marriage or homosexuality, but who among us can claim to be absolutely pure in matters sexual? Jesus' words, 'Let the one who is without sin be the first to cast a stone', are therefore timely reminders of our own frailty. How easy it is for us to make moral judgements, while forgetting the real people who such judgements affect. Jesus is our model here. He did not condemn the sinner, but neither did he condone the sin. Jesus reminds us that people are capable of reform if they are given opportunity. The Church must be a community of grace, a community free from legalism, a community who will not condemn but who will love.

The Beheading of John the Baptist

Sermon preached by Paul Walker at St Wilfrid's Church, Moorside, Sunderland, on Passion Sunday, 16 March 1997.

The Revd Paul Walker, 34, is a priest at the coalface of mission in the Church of England. He is priest-in-charge of the new Anglican church of St Wilfrid's, which meets in the Benedict Biscop primary school at Moorside. Nearly all the congregation of 120 are completely new to churchgoing. The church is a 'local ecumenical partnership', and Paul is also an accredited Methodist minister. He is regularly baptizing and confirming adult worshippers into both denominations. He and his wife Penny, who edits books with Routledge, moved with their two daughters to Moorside in June 1993. The church was started with a big Christmas service that year, after Paul spent six months visiting every home in the area. Sunderland is counted one of the poorest cities in Europe, but by local standards the church is on an estate that is largely middle class. The Christian message appealed to large numbers of teachers, government and other white-collar workers living there. More than 260 turned up for that first service and by Easter 300 were attending. Then numbers fell to 60 people and are now building back up again. This is a normal pattern for new churches. Paul, who plays cricket and golf and does the occasional Pause for Thought on BBC Radio 2, had a 'horrible feeling' at the age of 13 that he would one day be a vicar, but did not respond immediately. 'Through my teenage years I was looking for something,' he says. 'I tried everything – sex, drugs, rock and roll – I even tried Buddhism. But I found myself one day reading the Bible, something I had never done before. I found the figure of Jesus remarkably appealing and interesting.' By the time he was at Durham University, he was a committed Christian, but he resisted his vocation to the end. 'I wanted to earn money. At my selection conference I made sure I smoked like a chimney, got drunk and swore a lot. I just wanted it to go away, but I got accepted. I was quite annoyed.' He preaches once a week, and con-

fesses to enjoying it. 'I am a bit of a drama queen and like standing up at the front there. I like playing with words. My aim in preaching is to help people think in different ways about the life they are living at the moment. I want to help people see there is something in the Bible worth investigating for themselves.'

Texts: Mark 6.14–29 (The beheading of John the Baptist)
Bible: New International Version

We're continuing to look today at St Mark's Gospel, with the account of John the Baptist's death. Here is a story in a story, the story of a man dying for his principles, in the middle of a story of another man dying for his principles.

Every time I think about John the Baptist I feel vaguely uncomfortable, whether it is his anger when he calls people broods of vipers, or his extreme way of life, or here at his death. Look at this story. It has all the taboos of our modern society. Here we have a ruler – politics. We have a prophet – religion. We have a provocative dance – sex. And we have a beheading – death. There is even a hint of incest. There's something here to offend everybody.

There is a famous piece of graffiti which says: 'John the Baptist was the first Rotarian.' I'm not sure whether that is a criticism of John or the Rotary Club. Either way, John does not fit in well with our idea of a comfortable religion. And let's face it, a comfortable religion is often what we really want. We want a religion that helps us to get through this life. We want a religion that makes things easier. It's because of this that we can all love gentle Jesus, meek and mild. We can sympathize with tempestuous Peter who behaves like us. We can see in doubting Thomas a man struggling to believe like we often do and we can even grudgingly admire self-righteous Paul. But John the Baptist? The message of John to our modern world and today's Church is about as socially appropriate to a comfortable religion as a French kiss is to a family reunion.

The story we've just heard is simple. John has been thrown into prison because he said it was unlawful for Herod to marry his brother's wife. The law that John refers to is in fact a couple of verses taken from the book of Leviticus. This is the same book that tells us how to sprinkle the blood of turtledoves and how to wash ourselves when we've accidentally touched a dead body. These are hardly central tenets, even of the Old Testament, and not in the same league as the Ten Commandments.

Anyway, worrying about obscure details from the Old Testament is usually something we associate with the Pharisees. We Christians live by grace, not law, we say. And I can't be the only one who feels that there were surely more important things to worry about in first-century Palestine than who was sleeping with who at the palace. The same could be said for twentieth-century Britain. But John believed Herod's actions were wrong and said so. He suffered as a result. Others, maybe even the Pharisees themselves, realized that this was not a battle that was likely to be won. So they kept quiet.

Now let's not criticize the people who kept quiet. They were displaying a quality we all believe in: discretion, the better part of valour. We encourage it, we all want to keep the peace. But discretion was not one of John's virtues. Those who said nothing about Herod's marriage were behaving like us. In fact, they were behaving amazingly like our own English Church. For example, everybody tells the Church to encourage lifelong marriage, stop families breaking down, but nobody wants us to get personal. No one wants us to mention the family problems at the end of the Mall in London. The problems of our society must always be blamed on unknown strangers, not on those we know and care about.

When people read about teenage problems in Sunderland, they might think that Sunderland parents do not know how to bring up their kids. We know that's nonsense. The problem families do not live in areas like Moorside, they're in Pennywell. Yet if you talk to people in Pennywell they'll tell you that the problem families all live in two streets, and I bet that in those two streets they all blame a few houses. Society's problems can all be blamed on people elsewhere, and racism is the easiest option of all. And when it comes to the Church, we want the benefits of religion, not the costs. We want the Church to help us, not to challenge us. We want God to change other people to make our lives better, but we do not want him to change us for their sakes.

John made life difficult. John did not simply attack the general problem. John was not just against sin, that's easy. John made it specific, he made it personal and unfortunately for himself he made it royal. He must have had friends who said: 'Listen John,

I know Herod should not be doing that, but get on with baptizing people in the Jordan. You're not going to change the old fox now.' Sensible advice, but not heeded. John did not retract. He ended up in prison and ultimately headless for his pains.

Looking back we can all say how brave he was. How great it was that John held true to his convictions. How wonderful it is that he was vindicated when Jesus said that no mother's son has ever been greater than John the Baptist. He is a kind of first-century anti-hero. But let's be honest about this, it didn't do a great deal for him. I can see in John the Baptist a brave hero. I am left here with someone I can look up to and respect, but John ended up dead. What's the use of being remembered by history if it kills you? Would I want to be beheaded even if I knew that some obscure preacher two thousand miles away would admire me in two thousand years' time? I don't think so.

Every generation has thrown up similar heroes to John. People who have stood alone against the powers that be and have had nobody, or very few people, to support them. Most of them of course are anonymous because those who killed them don't want us to know about it. But we have a few heroes still. There was Galileo, who realized that Copernicus had been right that the earth went round the sun and not the other way round. He was forced to retract by the Inquisition and died a lonely man under house arrest. Thomas More dared to question another king marrying and then divorcing his brother's wife, when others knew that Henry VIII was not one to take criticism lightly. Thomas also lost his head. Dietrich Bonhoeffer, the German pastor, realized that Hitler's regime was evil. He was implicated and after lonely years in prison when he refused to retract was hanged just before the end of the war. All these people and many thousands like them stood alone. They were persecuted, yet they continued to stand for what they believed in and history has proved that they were right. Yet they paid a terrible price in their own lifetimes for standing up for the truth.

At the moment when you hear the news and you learn that people are dying in the anarchy that is Albania, be sure that among them are those who have died because they have stood against injustice, because they have put truth and right before themselves. In these situations, when food is scarce, there will always be those who stand up to the ones with guns demanding that food should be shared, and they are often killed. And they won't be remembered. What is right has cost them everything.

When I read about these people it is often with a sense of tragedy. With these people we don't have the satisfaction of knowing that they saw their argument being won. Gandhi was assassinated, but at least he saw the dawn of an independent India. Martin Luther King was shot, but he saw the birth of the civil rights movement. Countless eastern bloc dissidents saw the Berlin Wall come down. But there are so many who never live to see their dreams being fulfilled. They do what they do because truth, justice and what they believe to be right are more important to them than their own comfort and happiness.

And that is why John the Baptist is an uncomfortable subject to me. Because as a preacher I long to tell you that being part of the Church, having the Christian faith, is not simply pie in the sky when you die, but that it can improve your life now. Yet here is this man who lived in uncomfortable clothes, on a disgusting diet, in an inhospitable desert and ended his life in a prison cell before being beheaded. I long to say that such people were 'then' and that 'now' is different. But for some people it is not. We still need our John the Baptists. We still need people who will stand up for what they believe to be right, despite persecution from those in authority and ridicule from everybody else.

Our only problem is that we don't know who these people are. Only a few years ago the green lobby was written off as knit-your-own-muesli fanatics. Yet they stuck to their guns and now we're all green – or so we're being told constantly. But who are the John the Baptists today? Most likely, today's John the Baptists are the people I ridicule. Most likely they are the loonies who we all laugh at. It is the ethical or religious or political extremists whose ideas we mock that are often those who set tomorrow's agenda. Political freedom, democracy, sexual and racial equality were all ridiculous ideas at one time, but because people stood alone and sacrificed themselves, we reap the benefits.

We are left enjoying things that others suffered for and often died for. But for them there was simply death. And for many radicals that is simply it. For many people, life is snuffed out for the sake of a cause and it is accepted because the cause is greater than the individual, that 'the ends justify the means', and that death may be worth it. But I can't go along with that. I believe that each individual life also matters.

So let's go back to John the Baptist, the story we heard today, the story of a death which did not change anything, which comes in the middle of another story. That story is the Gospel. And the Gospel is almost the story of a death which didn't change anything. Except that, for those who accept it, the Gospel is the story of a death that changed everything.

In the scheme of that story, the death of John the Baptist is not only a victory for the truth, it is also a victory for John himself. It is the knowledge that self-sacrifice can lead to eternal victory which has led Christians to be brave and self-sacrificial in every generation. Yes, the story of John is uncomfortable, partly because it should disturb us into action and partly because it only has a happy ending because we believe in pie in the sky. But put another way, I believe in justice. I believe that goodness will be rewarded. Otherwise the world has no sense, no meaning. Without a belief that John reaped the benefits of keeping to his convictions, then to me he was brave but he was a brave fool.

I suppose that what I'm trying to say is that the story of John the Baptist is a tragedy. But the story of the Gospel is a victory. And the victory of the Gospel makes all tragedies like John's victories. Or put more simply still, at the heart of the Christian faith is a happy ending.

Felicity Amid the Flood

Sermon preached by Claire Wilson at a wedding at St Peter's Church, Belsize Park, London, on Sunday 15 December 1996.

The Revd Claire Wilson, 54, has recently become team vicar at All Saints, Chingford, Essex, after 9 years at St Peter's, Belsize Park. She has just stepped down as a part-time prison chaplain at Holloway. Before ordination she was a teacher of religious education and German at a comprehensive school in Hampstead. In 1966, for one year, she sold ladies' elastic stockings. Claire grew up in an extreme evangelical environment and during her teenage years she rejected the 'narrowness' she found there and spent some years searching for spiritual answers. In 1973, her first son was born after a difficult labour with a mental disability. That triggered a renewed interest in God, Christianity, liturgy and worship and in 1982 she was licensed as a Reader in the Church of England. She felt an increasingly strong vocation to the priesthood and in 1987 was ordained deacon by the then Bishop of London, the Right Revd Graham Leonard, who strongly opposes women priests and has since become a priest in the Roman Catholic Church. Claire was priested in St Paul's in 1994 as one of the first women priests in London. She preaches nearly every week, and prepares by looking at the readings for the day. 'I look for an unusual entry into the text and a way to take people by surprise,' she says. 'I prepare, not by sitting at a desk, but by walking around the streets. I am always on foot, I don't drive.' She reads from a text, but during her training at Salisbury she learned how to do this without looking as though that is what she was doing. She preaches for about 8 minutes, and writes her sermons out in pen and ink. A radical feminist in her theology, she aims not to give her congregation answers, but to provoke questions and new lines of enquiry. She also enjoys the act of preaching. 'I am human and I like the performance element,' she says. 'It is quite a heady feeling to stand there and feel that you have people's attention, that you have the power to entertain and to move them. I feel com-

fortable in the pulpit, I like to be there. It is a natural habitat for me.' She entered the award because she relishes competitions. 'I thought it would be good fun.'

Texts: Felicity amid the flood: A sermon on the occasion of the marriage of Julia and Peter.
Bible: New Revised Standard Version

Water, wickedness and survival in unlikely conditions: if you didn't expect to encounter the tale of Noah and his ark at this wedding – well, neither, till last week, did I. As a Bible reading it's the kind of last-minute unconventional idea that those of us who know Julia and Peter might expect them to hit upon. It's also, I believe, an inspired choice for our purposes today.

We relish stories like this in which frail human beings survive against dramatic odds. OK, the ark has been carefully built to divine specifications, but the conditions in which it needs to stay afloat will put even the Almighty's design to the test. And if the rising waters outside the ark present a challenge, what about the privations and problems inside? The writer of Genesis doesn't gratify our curiosity about the quality of life below deck, but subsequent imagination has filled in at least some gaps for us. One novel based on Noah's adventures highlights the delicate problems surrounding the animals' sleeping arrangements. Species disposed to eat each other could not be billeted in adjacent suites.

A handbuilt craft challenged by formidable elements without and logistical problems within – some of us may feel that the ark serves very well as an illustration of marriage, that holy estate into which Peter and Julia come now to be joined. Certainly marriage, like all arrangements human beings make for living together, is as fragile as any pre-technological construction of gopherwood. We may be sure that Peter and Julia will encounter, sooner or later, the floodwaters of adversity from without. They will also experience the tensions which inevitably arise from within when creatures with diverse habits and needs live together at close quarters: where that's concerned, cheetahs and antelopes have nothing on human beings!

But the ark, in spite of all this, survives: it does the job it was built for. And Noah and his crew seem to realize instinctively that all will be well. They do not underestimate the hazards, but they do have faith in the essential seaworthiness of their vessel. After all, this is not just any project; it has divine backing. It's God, we recall, who shuts the doors and cuts the mooring ropes.

And this project that we're caught up in today, this 'launching' of Julia and Peter which is both hilarious and holy, lighthearted and awesome, has more than ordinary backing. We are all here, for a start; our love, our goodwill and support will help them stay afloat! And Julia and Peter, we believe, have made their own preparations. They are embarking both with due respect for the fragility of their craft and with well-founded confidence that it will withstand the elements.

What's more, of course, the story of Noah is not just an exercise in survival. God puts him and his family into the ark for a purpose. When the assorted voyagers step out on to dry land again, they encounter a changed world, a world newborn, recreated with all the freshness and beauty of the First Day. They emerge into a world that has been given a second chance, the opportunity to start again with new prospects for harmony between creatures and Creator.

Life on board the ark will test and change Julia and Peter, remodel and shape them, break them and make them. From the deck of their vessel they will look out through new eyes: and that will go some small way to changing the world. What more need we say then except God bless you – and bon voyage!

And for the Love of You

Sermon preached by Brenda Woods at Crowland Methodist Church on 5 January 1997 and subsequently at Deeping St Nicholas.

The Revd Brenda Woods, 52, had expected as a probationer to be sent to the inner city. Instead she found herself in the Lincolnshire Fens. Her first career was as a physics teacher in a comprehensive school in Battersea, South London, where she came the head of science and then a senior teacher. Her call to the ministry came out of a spiritual crisis and months of depression. 'I was unhappy at work, church and home and there was nothing left,' she says. 'Then came this weird idea of being a Methodist minister, which I though I couldn't possibly do because I didn't really believe in God and all I did was cry.' After a month of wishing it would go away, she finally discussed it with her minister who advised her that the call sounded authentic. She became a local preacher, then 'candidated' or went through the Methodist selection process. When asked why she wanted to be a minister, she replied: 'I don't, but I am passionately interested in worship, pastoral care and spirituality and I am willing to leave it to others to decide if ministry is the best way for me.' She trained at Wesley House, Cambridge, and was then allowed to spend a year at the Roman Catholic Institute for Spriritual Leadership in Chicago. In 1994, she was sent as a probationer to the Peterborough circuit. To prepare a sermon she prays with the lectonary readings and thinks about it all week, often while shopping or mowing the lawn. She reads commentaries and newspapers for ideas. She is trying to reduce her reliance on notes when preaching to become 'more open to the Spirit'. On Friday she gets a 'sinking feeling' when she is convinced she has nothing worth saying. By Saturday she cannot think of anything else to say, and she takes the plunge to trust in God. She enjoys the satisfaction of a sermon well preached, a job well done. 'I am trying to challenge people to think about how they live their faith,' she says. 'I hope I am comforting

*them as well.' Her depression is something that can still come and go.
'My experience has been that God is there in the darkness and usually when I look back on a time of depression, it is a time when faith
has grown. I think sometimes that seeds always grow in the dark.'*

Texts: Deuteronomy 29.10–15; Jeremiah 31.31–34; Luke
22.14–20

Bible: Jerusalem

Shadowlands is a film that requires a box of tissues by your
side – a story of love replacing legalism, of heart winning
over mind and habit, of the old being replaced by the new of
lives being radically changed through love.

Two confirmed bachelors have their lives turned upside down
by a vivacious American woman who is not afraid to speak her
mind. Joy Gresham writes to C.S. Lewis because she and her
young son enjoy his books. She visits him in England and a
friendship begins. Jack and his brother continually reassure each
other that nothing will change as a result of friendship, that there
is no need to get involved. Returning to London after her
divorce she asks Jack to marry her so that she can remain in
England with her son Douglas. It is to be purely a marriage of
convenience with no strings attached. There need be no commitment for Jack. They will see each other infrequently. His life can
remain as it was, unaffected by this marriage.

It is only when Joy's cancer is diagnosed that Jack realizes how
deeply he is affected by her suffering and likely death and thus
how he has come to love her and how much she has loved him,
as we suspected, from the beginning. So now Jack asks her to
marry him; this time because they are in love and both of them
want to. The love of this marriage enables what the formality of
the first could not. Jack's life changes for ever, he is committed to
her, he gets involved with her, he welcomes her into his life and
his home. His happiness is now bound up with her. Jack has discovered within himself depths of passion and desire and love and
anguish that he never dreamt possible.

Where do you fit into this story in your relationship with your
God who has always loved you? Are you like those two brothers,
determined nothing will change your lifestyle. Anxious that your
relationship with God will not upset your life. Or perhaps you

are like Jack after his first marriage to Joy. You have entered into a formal relationship with God, yet you do not want to get involved in any real way, you are unaware of how much you are loved and you do not feel much love for God yourself.

Or maybe you are like Jack, after Joy's cancer is discovered, realizing the depth of feeling within yourself and finding that God has loved you all along. So now you want to enter into a new relationship based on love and your desire to be committed. The response of love to love, of heart to heart. Thus you welcome God into your life. Your happiness is bound up in your relationship with God. Your life changes radically and in ways you never imagined possible.

Is Jack's story everyone's story? It is certainly the story of Israel. We heard in those Bible readings of Israel's first covenant with God, a covenant initiated by God but misunderstood and continually broken by the people. Then Jeremiah speaks of the new covenant which will be different because it will be based on love, it will be written in their hearts. It is to be heart stuff – no longer only head stuff.

At the Last Supper with his disciples, Jesus raises a glass of wine and invites them to drink to this new covenant that is about to be made possible by his approaching death. It is through Jesus that this new intimate relationship of love with God can happen; this relationship that was not possible through the formality of the old law and the old covenant. For love enables what formality never could – a dedication, commitment, self-giving, a willingness to have one's life changed by God, to live dependent on God.

The covenant prayer in the Methodist Covenant service is John Wesley's way of describing this new relationship:

> I am no longer my own but yours.
>
> Put me to what you will, rank me with whom you will; put me to doing, put me to suffering; let me be employed for you or laid aside for you, exalted for you or brought low for you; let me be full, let me be empty, let me have all things, let me have nothing; I fully and freely yield all things to your pleasure and disposal.

We can see how this describes Jesus' relationship with his Father, a relationship in which Jesus is able to abandon himself to the Father. And that is only possible because Jesus knows how much he is loved by the Father. That sort of relationship is one we too can have. It is the promise of Jesus. Gone is the need for a formal, legal marriage. Now there can be a marriage of love.

I hope you read that very moving article in our church newsletter in which Helen describes that formal relationship: the being a member, the going to church for years, yet the lack of love. All head stuff – no heart stuff! And then Helen tells of the movement towards the heart, the growing relationship of love. So Jack's story is Helen's story.

Perhaps Jack's story is everyone's story, for are we not all making that journey from the head to the heart, the journey towards God in which head and heart come to balance each other? And I guess none have yet arrived! It is a journey in which more and more we experience for ourselves the love of God which is poured out for us, which is drawing us into an ever deeper and more intimate relationship – a love into which we can increasingly trust ourselves and through which our lives are changed.

Love is the key. John Wesley realized that without love the covenant is impossible for us, and so before this covenant prayer comes perhaps the most important phrase: 'and for the love of you'. And for the love of you – without the experience of God's love this is all duty on our part.

'I fully and freely yield all things to your pleasure and disposal.' All things? No way. Not out of duty. But out of love? Ah! Yes! If there is love, love received and love given, then all things become possible. If our response comes out of our deep sense of being loved by God then, and only then, can I truly say: 'I am no longer my own but yours.'

It is our Methodist tradition to renew our covenant with God each year. It offers us an opportunity to examine our relationship with God. If yours is a formal, legal sort of relationship then doubtless you will find this covenant prayer difficult to say. Maybe you will leave bits out! If you are in the process of discovering there is more – so very much more than you ever dreamt – if you have begun to experience for yourself that God loves you with passion and desires only the best for you, then you can throw yourself into this new covenant with gay abandon. For the heart can offer what the head cannot. The heart can say: 'I love you, I'll go anywhere, I'll do anything for you. Is your heart ready for this?'

The Living Legend

Sermon preached by Thomas Woodsend at morning service at St Columba's Church, Kilmacolm, Renfrewshire, on Remembrance Sunday, 1990.

Thomas Woodsend, 81, grandfather of seven, is a reader in the Greenock presbytery of the Church of Scotland and has preached in about 20 churches in the district. He might preach as many as 30 or as few as six times a year, 'depending on how many ministers break a leg just before a service'. Congregations in his district average at 250. Sadly, he has recently had to turn down invitations because of worsening asthma, which also forced him to withdraw from the final stages of this award. His youth was spent in the army, in Africa, Italy and North-West Europe. At 30 he went into private business. He started off sweeping the floor and finished up as chairman of a light engineering company with a staff of 300 in the west of Scotland, taking early retirement to go to Glasgow University as a student of divinity. He and his wife, Mary, have just celebrated their golden wedding anniversary, and he says his hobby is 'to walk around pretending to be a minor prophet'. He spends from half an hour to three hours preparing his sermons, and although he preaches with a draft in front of him, he does not always stick to it. 'I usually preach until everybody's asleep, which takes about fifteen minutes. I enjoy being able to talk without interruption, the feeling that I can offer people something they can take or leave, some significant thought.'

Once a week six elderly gentlemen go up to their golf club, not to play golf – for if any one of them did play a few holes his drives would no longer soar like a rocket down the fairway – but just to have coffee together. They recall old struggles and hopes for the future, they talk and listen and support each other. Together, they have about them the air of a mellow autumn afternoon.

Sometimes one of them, the youngest, finds himself in a chair opposite the fireplace. When that happens his mind can wander, for above the fireplace is a small plaque, and on that plaque are the names of members of the club who were killed in the Second World War. Several of them were at school with him. One indeed was his closest friend, a boy with whom he went camping in the holidays and whom he could still visualize waiting for him on the first tee. Now, fifty years later, he himself was sitting in the clubhouse drinking coffee. Like many of those who returned he had very mixed feelings – personal sadness, thankfulness at having himself survived the war, but tinged with guilt at having lived when his friends and members of his family had died, and not certain that he had done very much in return.

Today, fewer and fewer people can have this reaction for the two world wars are fading into the past like the Wars of the Roses, and later wars will follow them. Why then is it that we still keep Remembrance Sunday? Is it not time for us to forgive and forget? Is it to thank God again for victory? We are sure that we were morally right, and in consequence God must have been on our side and decreed that we would win. What makes us uneasy is that the other side believed that they were right and worshipped the same God, and were certain that if by chance they were defeated the Lord would raise them up again. As children of God, moreover, we might all have been sitting in church together.

Enemies in the field can often find a common humanity. After the fighting had stopped in the Falkland Islands the main reaction of our troops was not one of joy in victory, but of relief that it was over and sadness for all the loss of life. One thinks of the small incident in the First World War when the Germans held aloft from their trenches a board on which was written 'The French are fools.' It was shot to pieces. The next day they put up another, 'The British are fools.' It was shot to pieces. On the third day another appeared, 'We are all fools, let us go home.' Not a shot was fired.

Some people have an idea that we wear poppies and keep Remembrance Sunday in order to glorify war and to let old men look back through rosy spectacles to the past, but I cannot think of anything further from the truth. Why then do we still keep it?

We keep it to remember those who, in desperate defence of our freedom died that we should not let it happen again. And not only those who died, but those on both sides who suffered the long ache of bereavement, the child who would never see a parent, the woman who suddenly realized that her husband would never be coming back to her.

We keep it as a duty to those who fought and did come back, wounded or injured and who now in their old age need our help. We keep it to reflect on the ghastliness of war and, if we can, pass some of that feeling on to the next generation who knew nothing of it and who, having sat through the drama of war films, may sometimes wish that they too had some way in which to prove themselves. To remember that war is a sad and dirty business, of setting each other's cities on fire, of digging into the rubble and pulling out the burnt and mangled remains of women and children, and of losing all faith in any God who could allow such things to happen.

We may say that death goes on all the time. People die doing very brave things. They die in accidents, on the roads, in all sorts of places. What is special about deaths in war? The answer is that these were deaths for the community. Without that bitter harvest, you and I would not be here today. The community must remember those who saved it for many of those who did so no longer have anyone else to remember them.

Finally – and this is most important – we keep it in the hope that these things, our annual remembrance, former enemies coming together and sharing in sorrow, will bring hopes and efforts for peace – just as Christ on the cross was an instrument for peace. Those in brief are the reasons why in an act of tribal unity we remember those who fell in the wars.

Now let us put this matter of remembrance into a wider framework. Each of us has our different sorts of remembrance. There are our private memories, the things which give us roots. They can be conjured up by all sorts of things: a photograph, a lock of hair, a dream, an old hairbrush, or just our passing thoughts. They are what we hang on to. One of the most pathetic sights in the war was a stream of refugees, each with a few sad possessions, an old kettle, a doll, a teddybear, keeping a link if they could with the past.

Each of us also draws from a tribal memory, what Jung called the group unconscious, in which lie the shadowy traces of what happened to our ancestors. Bear in mind that each of us comes from the mating of thousands of humans before us and before that of creatures who swung from the trees. And in our biological make-up are to be found links with species long extinct. Like them we shall not pass this way again.

Out of this stream of evolution there emerged, at a fairly late stage, the gift first of curiosity and then of self-awareness, awareness of ourselves. We, homo sapiens, are probably the only species that can look at itself in its own situation. If you take a horse to water it will not study its reflection and say: 'Well, look at that now – I'm a horse.' But you and I can do that. I don't mean that we should splash about in a puddle of water and say that we are horses. I mean that we can look at ourselves with detachment.

When we look at ourselves it is inevitable that we should wonder who we are and how we got here. And this is not just curiosity but part of our search for psychological security. To feel secure one has to have roots of some sort, and if we do not have them we shall make them up. Some of these roots may be drawn from historical fact, but if that is not enough we shall draw on our memories, conscious and unconscious, and on our imagination, and weave these together into myth and legend. That is what brings meaning to our lives. That, so far as we are concerned, is our past.

Let us take, for example, some of the stories in the Bible. And if I use the word 'myth' I do not necessarily mean that the story is untrue. I mean that it conveys a meaning. Adam and Eve, Noah and the flood, the cloak of Elijah – we draw deeply on these for our faith. But bear in mind that their historical accuracy, what would have been recorded on a camera, is of much less importance than the meaning which they bring us as myth and legend, for it is surely in our finding the meaning underneath that the Spirit shapes our faith. You and I may live in history, but to find a meaning we also live in myth. Those who died in the wars are a very important and heroic part of that myth, with all the other things which bring meaning to our lives, which stir the imagination, sometimes perhaps a little noble or dramatic, or deeply felt, a touch of compassion, a search for the good. Some day our myth will be legend.

You and I can find inspiration in legends of long ago. But we must also reach out into the future. Those who come after us will in turn seek their legends of long ago. What they find will be what we do today. What will that legend about us be? In 2,000 years we may have reached the stars but people will still have the same curiosity about their own roots and tell their children the stories of those who lived long ago. Will they dig in our valleys and find our little bits and pieces and work out how we lived? Will they look at the ancient ruins of our churches, sinking by then into the ground, and wonder what sort of a God was once worshipped there?

Let us hope that they will find the legend of a people who fought only when they had to; a people who remembered those who died in order to preserve their freedom; a people of compassion who did not forget those, on both sides, who had lost their loved ones. Let them find in us a vision of a man who, two thousand years before, had taught by the Sea of Galilee, a people who, in following him did their best to act justly, to love mercy, and to walk humbly with their God.

A Humble Heart

The winning sermon preached by William Anderson at Southwark Cathedral in the final of the 1996 'Preacher of the Year' award in November 1996.

Father William Anderson, 66, Canon of St Mary's Cathedral in Aberdeen, was the only Roman Catholic to make the shortlist of 30 last year. He read classics at Edinburgh and Cambridge Universities before studying for six years in Rome, where he was ordained in 1960. He taught for 8 years at St Mary's College, Blairs, near Aberdeen, and worked for the BBC religious department in Edinburgh from 1969 to 1977 and then as spiritual director at the Scots College in Rome. He was also Catholic chaplain to Aberdeen University from 1986 to 1993. He was clearly flabbergasted to win the award and later described it as an ordeal he had no wish to repeat. He always gets nervous before preaching and had been the first to go on because the final was taken in alphabetical order. At the time, in an interview with The Scotsman, *he said: 'I had not dressed up. I was just in my suit and I suddenly discovered they wanted us to wear some robe or other. I had to borrow an Anglican cassock for the occasion. One felt rather like an inadequate soloist, sitting through Beethoven's* Ninth *and then making a hash of the vocal part at the end. The tension was dreadful.' A year later, however, he says: 'It came at the time as a great surprise to me, but it was a great delight and a tremendous honour. I hope and pray it has made no difference to anything in terms of my preaching, but it could not but give me a bit more confidence and assurance that what I had been trying to do was apparently along the right lines. It was a very, very happy experience. Preaching has an essential role. For the great majority of churchgoers it is the only kind of help and guidance and instruction they receive, week by week. A good sermon should give them encouragement, hope and a sense of enjoyment in their faith.' Appropriately, his winning sermon was on 'humility'.*

Texts: Psalm 51

The sacrifice of God is a troubled spirit. A broken
and contrite heart, O God, thou shalt not despise.

Bible: Authorised

Fifty years ago, at school in Edinburgh, my class started to
read Chaucer. One of the early lines in the Prologue runs: 'In
Southwark at the Tabard as I lay.' I haven't given Southwark
much thought in the meantime, but much of the Prologue has
stayed in my mind – about that band of pilgrims setting out
from here to Canterbury six hundred years ago and telling their
tales. Oh, the Friar, the Pardoner and others show little evidence
of broken and contrite hearts; yet in many of the pilgrims there
are points of character, now haughty, now humble, where we
probably recognize ourselves! Only the poor Parson and his
brother the Ploughman escape the author's satire.

It was a real ploughman of a later time, Robert Burns, who
visited his ridicule upon those he thought were hypocrites, espe-
cially in matters of religion. Here, for instance, is the dissem-
bling Holy Willie addressing his Maker:

> I bless and praise thy matchless might
> When thousands thou hast left in night
> That I am here afore thy sight
> For gifts an' grace,
> A burning and a shining light
> To a' this place.

And the poem's title? 'Holy Willie's Prayer'! And we think, how
droll! Yet it is perfectly possible for us to delude ourselves even
when we pray. Father Jock Dalrymple, that exemplary Scottish
priest, came to suspect, after many years of ministry, that he had
been more in love with prayer than with God. Probably we too
have preferred at times to take centre stage and consign the
Almighty to the wings.

The battle goes on, in all of us, between pride and humility,
and the lines can be blurred at times, the vice seeming almost to
be the virtue. The devil knows what he is about. Screwtape and
his henchmen dislike unemployment! Remember that line in
Genesis: 'now the serpent was more subtle than any beast of the
field'? When we protest we are of no account, or that we are mis-

ery itself and nothing but refuse, how would we like to be taken at our word and have this said of us by others?

A waggish friend, an Anglican, remarked to me recently: 'Yes, I do so admire humility – in other people!' And so perhaps do you and I. After all, to have our hearts bruised or crushed could involve a degree of discomfort – even pain – which we would rather do without! A troubled spirit, a humble, contrite heart: how elusive it is for the honest seeker, how hard to discern. Hilaire Belloc's epigram fairly hits the mark:

> I said to Heart: how goes it? Heart replied:
> Right as a Ribstone Pippin; but it lied.

I remember an eminent cardiologist opening a talk with this word from Jeremiah: 'The heart is deceitful above all things; who can know it?' This is surely as true of the spiritual as of the physical side.

The author of Psalm 51 – possibly Kind David repenting of his adultery with Bathsheba – the author has a series of telling insights into the affairs of the heart. And he comes before God with a number of stark imperatives: have mercy, blot out, wash me, purge me, and so on. There's urgency as well as realism about his highly personal prayer, self-abasement included. Yes, just occasionally it is proper almost to grovel as he does when we pray; to come before the Almighty, slime of that earth that each of us is, an admit: 'Lord, my name is mud!' His conviction of the need for drastic measures led John Donne to cry out:

> Batter my heart, three-personed God, for you
> As yet but know, breathe, shine, and seek to mend,
> That I may rise and stand, o'erthrow me, and bend
> Your force to break, blow, burn and make me whole.

Indeed our sin is ever before us, so is our waywardness, our dallying with temptation. The battering ram of God's insistent love alone will crush our underlying pride.

For all that, humility should not make permanent door mats of us, mud or no mud! It should not oblige us to think less of ourselves than of others, or have a low opinion of our gifts. Perfect humility would not mean freedom from thinking about ourselves one way or the otehr at all! Disinterest in self would lead us to focus our thinking and our acting on the needs of other people, for humility is charity's first cousin. St Francis de Sales, for all his *douceur*, teases us about our self-importance even at surface level: 'Some people are proud,' he declares, 'because they ride a fine horse, or have a feather in their hat, or are very well dressed. This is obvious folly, for if there is any glory here it belongs to the horse or the bird or the tailor!'

Psalm 51 is an exercise in self-examination, transparently candid. The desire to be cleansed is intense, for the consciousness of sin oppresses its author. 'Wash me thoroughly,' he begs, 'create in me a clean heart.' And the whole poem, in its prayerful power, challenges us in our struggle to be open, to be lowly in God's sight. And it sets before us, with a rising degree of optimism, ideals that would be within our grasp, if only we would put ourselves meekly in God's hands, if only we would trust his loving kindness. Neither burnt offering nor any other external show of service will suffice. Only a troubled spirit, only a change of heart will do. And with delicious diffidence the psalmist is hopeful that God will not despise his bruised, repentant being. A lovely touch of courtesy this, arising from his penitence.

Mind you, we can spend so much time in trying to eliminate the great 'I am' that we may become vainly anxious, even scrupulous about it. Humour is a helpful corrective. So I like to remember the seventeenth-century Scottish peer, Lord Erskine, who complained to his publisher about the tardy production of his autobiography. He was told that the printers had sadly run out of capitals 'I's!

If we have found our text, our psalm useful, if its message and beauty have moved us, we should make it our own, commit it to memory. The investive C.S. Lewis tells us of this habit of 'festooning' his prayers with personal thoughts that bring out the force of originals for him. Scholarship, tradition, received piety, all have their place. But for you, for me, in our quest for forgiveness, only your heart, only mine, can individually respond. And, in so far as they *do* respond, we shall gradually inch our way forward to holiness.

Mercifully and from time to time there *are* saints among and around us – good, godly people in every walk of life. Their humility shines when it catches the light; the one who's affronted and feels it is no more than is deserved; the one who assumes the successful rival was the better choice for a promoted post; or who

will work with a will to the plans of others when they run con-
trary to his or her advice – and a hundred other instances. Saints
present and past – of Old and New Testament times – illumine in
great matters and in the small penitential twilight. Among them
is your London-born Thomas à Becket, whose shrine Chaucer's
pilgrims, and real pilgrims too, went to Canterbury, 'the holy,
blisful martyr to seke'. Consonant with our theme, pointing up
our text, are these words from T.S. Eliot's play about him: 'The
true martyr is he who has become the instrument of God, who
has lost his will in the will of God and who no longer desires anything for himself, not even the glory of being a martyr.'